Peter Lund Simmonds

Hops, their cultivation, commerce and uses in various countries

A manual of reference for the grower, dealer, and brewer

Peter Lund Simmonds

Hops, their cultivation, commerce and uses in various countries
A manual of reference for the grower, dealer, and brewer

ISBN/EAN: 9783744715157

Printed in Europe, USA, Canada, Australia, Japan

Cover: Foto ©Andreas Hilbeck / pixelio.de

More available books at **www.hansebooks.com**

HOPS;
THEIR CULTIVATION, COMMERCE, AND USES
IN VARIOUS COUNTRIES.

HOPS;

THEIR CULTIVATION, COMMERCE, AND USES IN VARIOUS COUNTRIES.

A MANUAL OF REFERENCE

FOR THE GROWER, DEALER, AND BREWER.

BY

P. L. SIMMONDS,

EDITOR OF THE JOURNAL OF APPLIED SCIENCE;
HON. AND CORRESPONDING MEMBER OF THE AGRICULTURAL SOCIETIES OF MONTREAL, CANADA;
THE PHILADELPHIA AND NEW ORLEANS SOCIETIES FOR PROMOTING AGRICULTURE;
THE AGRICULTURAL SOCIETY OF KONIGSBERG;
AND THE IMPERIAL AUSTRIAN AGRICULTURAL SOCIETY, ETC.

E. & F. N. SPON.
LONDON: 48, CHARING CROSS.
NEW YORK: 446, BROOME STREET.
1877.

PREFACE.

A LONG connection with agricultural literature, and an extensive home and foreign and colonial correspondence with cultivators and agricultural societies, have shown me how rapidly hop culture is extending with the increased demand for beer, and hence the necessity for some reliable manual of ready reference, bringing down the practice and statistics on this important product to the present time.

Although I cannot hope to be able to afford much practical or novel information to the experienced hop growers of England, yet this attempt on my part to condense into a reasonable compass a few useful hints and suggestions, combined with the latest statistics of production and consumption in various countries, may perhaps prove acceptable in some distant quarters, and especially in our Australian colonies.

P. L. SIMMONDS.

85, FINBOROUGH ROAD, S.W.

CONTENTS.

CHAPTER. I.

History, Botany, Economic Uses, and Chemistry of Hops .. .. Page 1

CHAPTER II.

Medicinal Uses and Preparations of Hops 18

CHAPTER III.

Systems of Cultivation practised or recommended 28

CHAPTER IV.

Cultivation of the Hop—*continued* 43

CHAPTER V.

Qualities and Keeping of Hops, and Statistics of Culture and Production in England 54

CHAPTER VI.

Cultivation and Production in European States 81

CHAPTER VII.

Hop Production on the American Continent .. .. Page 97

CHAPTER VIII.

Culture and Progress in Australasia 107

CHAPTER IX.

Bitter Substitutes which have been used for the Hop. Statistics of Imports and Prices of Foreign Hops. British and Foreign Beer Consumption, Malt, Brewing, &c. 124

HOPS.

CHAPTER I.

HISTORY, BOTANY, ECONOMIC USES, AND CHEMISTRY OF HOPS.

THE hop, so extensively cultivated here and in other countries for the use of the brewer, and so well known to every housekeeper for culinary use, was not unknown to the ancients, being mentioned by the Arabian physician Mesué, who lived about 845. Hops were apparently first used for beer in Germany and in the Dutch breweries about the year 1400, their properties and uses being well understood. It was introduced into England from Flanders in 1524, but its strobiles were not used to preserve English beer, until about the year 1600. Henry VIII., in 1530, forbade the breweries to mix hops in their beer, and somewhat later Parliament was petitioned by Londoners to prohibit their use, " as they would spoil the taste of the drink, and endanger the people."

Beckmann ('Hist. of Inv.,' vol. iv. p. 386) states that plantations of hops had begun to be formed in England A.D. 1552. They are first mentioned in the English Statute-book in that year, viz. in the 5th and 6th Edward VI., c. 5 (repealed 5 Eliz., c. 2), an Act directing that land formerly in tillage should again be so cultivated, but excepting, amongst other ground, " land set with saffron or hops ; " and by an Act of Parliament of the first year of James I., anno 1603, c. 18, it appears that hops were then produced in abundance in England.

In the oldest book I know about hops (Reynolde Scot's 'Perfite Platforme of a Hoppe Garden'), dated 1574, and printed in black letter, with many prefaces terminating in inverted pyramids of type, Kent is spoken of as the county of hops. The system of cultivation appears to have little changed since then ; and the book, if it were not written in the style of an Act of Parliament, and interlarded with moral reflections and allusions to every poet and orator of ancient times, might have been written in the present day. Yet hops, at that date, were but of recent cultivation. For ages, while our ancestors were wont to flavour their ale with ground ivy, and honey, and various bitters, a weed called " hop " had been known about the hedges of England ; but no one thought to cultivate it for brewing until the beginning of the sixteenth century. Some say the cultivated plant came first from Flanders, where it was certainly used before our brewers knew its virtues. In France, hop gardens are very ancient. Mention is made of them in some of the oldest records, though what the hops were used for does not appear. In England it had many enemies to contend with at first.

The leafy cone-like catkins or imbricated heads (strobili) of the common hop (*Humulus lupulus*, Lin.), a dioecious plant, with a perennial root, have long been an important article of commerce, and the culture and trade are becoming more and more extensive. The scales are scattered over with resinous spherical glands, which are easily rubbed off, and have a powerful agreeable odour and bitter taste; they appear to consist of an acid, ethereal oil, an aromatic resin, wax, extractive, and a bitter principle called lupuline. By pressure, hop heads yield a green, light, acrid oil, called oil of hops.

The aggregate fruits of this plant are botanically known under the name of strobiles, in common parlance as hops. These fruits consist of scales (bracts) and achaenia, the latter of which are surrounded by yellowish aromatic glands. They are usually termed lupulinic glands, and are the most active part of hops. They contain a volatile oil, and a bitter principle called *lupuline*, or *lupulite*, to the presence of which hops owe their properties. The bracts also contain some lupuline, and are therefore not devoid altogether of active principles. .

The female flowers, growing on a separate plant, are in the form of a catkin, having each pair of flowers supported by a bract, which is ovate, acute, tubular at base. Sepal solitary, obtuse, smaller than the bract, and enfolding the ovary. Ovary roundish, compressed; stigmas two, long, subulate, downy. The bracts enlarge into a persistent catkin, each bract enclosing a nut enveloped in its permanent bractlet, and several grains of yellow lupuline.

To the folioles or scales of the flower of the hop adhere a certain quantity of yellow powder or dust. Ives attributes to this powder alone the active principle of hops. But Payen and Chevallier are of opinion that the entire flower contains the same active principles which are found in the yellow dust. If this were not so, the hops, which in transport lose a great quantity of this yellow powder, would have but a feeble effect in the manufacture of beer.

As the quality of hops depends largely upon the amount of lupuline they contain, care is necessary to select those which have been fully matured on the vine before picking, when the lupuline will be found in much greater abundance, and of better quality. When derived from the fresh hop, it is of a very brilliant light lemon colour, almost transparent, and of a very strong aromatic odour. When rubbed between the fingers the grains are very easily broken, and adhere to the fingers, but on exposure to the light, or when from older hops, it becomes darker in colour, more opaque, and less gummy when rubbed between the fingers, according to the age. Owing to the difficulty of separating the powder from new hops (from the tendency it has to adhere to the scales, because of the resinous exudation with which it is coated, making its yield by mechanical process smaller), and the comparatively high price of new hops, as compared with old, making it less remunerative, the powder is mostly obtained from old hops. When the hop becomes old, the resinous exudation coating the lupuline concretes, and no longer adheres to the leaf, so that it can be easily separated by whipping the strobiles and sifting. When hops have become a year old, or as soon as the new crop comes into market, they are called old, and command only about one-half the price of the new crop. When two years old, they are called old-olds, and are still less valuable; and when five years old are considered worthless to brewers, although they still contain the lupuline, which possesses a part of its bitterness, but is destitute of volatile oil.

The age of hops can be told pretty accurately until they have attained three years; after that it is very doubtful.

During the first year they retain their bright green colour and fine, strong aromatic smell, and the lupuline is bright yellow.

The second year they become darker, more dead-like, losing their bright colour, and have a sweet, slightly cheesy odour, which is due to the oxidation of the volatile oil, converting it into valerianic acid. The lupuline is of a golden yellow colour.

The third year the colour is not much changed, but the odour becomes faint, with the same cheesy smell. The lupuline is of a dark yellow or reddish tint.

The female plant, which is the object of careful cultivation, on account of its bitter and odorous strobiles employed in brewing, is much richer in principles than the male plant, from which it is distinguished by its aromatic, tonic, and narcotic properties; qualities which are combined in no other substance.

Economic Uses of Hops.—The roots and the stem of this plant merit also attention, as they furnish a raw material, presenting the planter with a secondary useful product.

The roots removed with the plant in the course of plucking, and which are generally thrown away, not only contain a starchy substance, which may be converted into glucose and alcohol, but also a large proportion of tannin, which the tanneries might use with advantage. This substance also offers a good material for making excellent paper-pulp and cardboard.

The stem possesses useful qualities; vegetable wax can be obtained from it, also a sap from which a durable reddish-brown can be made, and its ash is used in the manufacture of the Bohemian glass. Like the roots, it furnishes a very solid pulp for paper and cardboard. The useful part of the stem is its textile fibre, which easily separates from the ligneous portion, after a steeping of two or three weeks, and of this fibre ropes and coarse fabrics of the greatest strength are made. After bleaching of the combed fibre, carpets with white and brown stripes have been made of it.

A M. Van der Scheldon recommended, in 1866, the following process for making a coarse cloth of good quality from the fibre of the hop. After the flowers have been gathered, the stalks are cut, made into bundles, and steeped like hemp. The maceration is the most important operation; for if it is not done with proper care, it is very difficult to separate the threads of the bark from the woody fibre. When the stalks have been well steeped, they are dried in the sun, beaten like hemp with a wooden mallet, and thus the threads are loosened easily. They are then carded, and are ready for weaving in the usual way. By this means a strong cloth is obtained. The thickest stalks also produce a thread suitable for the manufacture of rope.

The young sprouts or shoots, although slightly bitter, are sometimes cooked and eaten like asparagus; and the roots, according to Lindley, have been employed as a substitute for sarsaparilla.

A farmer in the north of France, having been driven by the scarcity of fodder to try to make use of whatever fell in his way for feeding his cattle, proved that hop leaves were a valuable element of food for cows when mixed with other substances. He found that whenever he gave them hop leaves he always obtained more milk, and his cows throve better than usual. The leaves must be used as soon as they are plucked, for the cows object to them when dried by the sun.

The hop bine has often been suggested as a paper material, but no practical action has yet been taken on any extensive scale in the matter.

In 1838, George Robert D'Harcourt included it in a patent among various other substances; and in the following year Thomas MacGauran also patented paper-making from hop bine, either by itself, or mixed with other suitable material. Again, in 1854, Thomas L. Holt and William Charlton obtained provisional protection for using the hop stem or bine with other plants, either alone or combined with rags.

In 1845, a patent was taken out for using spent hops from the breweries for paper-making.

An invention of Mr. Henry Dyer, of Camberwell, recently published, describes improvements in the manufacture of pulp for paper-making, and consists in the application and employment as materials for this purpose of spent hops or spent malt from breweries or distilleries, either together or separately, in combination or not with other materials, such as cotton, linen, hemp, woollen or silk rags, or esparto, diss, palm leaves, straw, wood pulp, jute, gunny, manilla, Indian grass, and waste paper.

The spent hops and malt, whether employed together or separately, and with or without the other substances referred to, are to be treated by the processes and machinery usually employed for boiling, pulping, and bleaching the ordinary materials used for paper-making, and when converted into pulp may be at once made into paper, or compressed and dried for sale as half-stuff.

Instead of spent hops, fresh hops may be used, in the case

of an over-abundant supply, or of a crop unfit for brewing purposes on account of blight or other causes.

The proportions of the different substances would be readily understood by paper-makers, and may be varied to suit their various requirements.

This invention claims to utilize materials hitherto valueless for any purpose except as a manure.

The claim protected by the patent is, the application and employment for the manufacture of pulp for paper-making of spent or fresh hops or spent malt, either alone or together, or in combination or not with other materials ordinarily used for paper-making.

At a meeting of paper-makers in France, in 1873, Messrs. Jourdeuil, Pauzot, and Gusses submitted samples of a textile material made from the bark of the hop stalk. By removing the outer skin, and subjecting it to chemicals, a textile substance was produced possessing length, suppleness, and delicacy of texture.

This is important to the hop farmer; for if the season should not prove favourable for the production of first-class hops, the paper-making material will compensate in some degree for this deficiency. No doubt the growth of hops will be introduced in future in many districts where they are not grown at present, as the large amount of material which they will supply for paper-making will alone ensure a good return for their cultivation.

The hop is also well known as a garden plant. It blossoms from June till August, and may be propagated by seed or by dividing the roots. It likes a deep, loamy soil, and is valuable as an ornamental climber over temporary arbours, trelliswork,

&c., in summer, as its leaves are very large and afford a fine shade. The "white bine" and the "grey bine" are the best sorts for this purpose; they succeed each other.

The flower, forming a spiked inflorescence, gives rise to scales, at the base of which the fruit is developed, protected against humidity by the resinous and very odoriferous powder of a golden yellow, named lupuline.

In a technical point of view, hops are the principal element in the brewing industry; but being very sensible to the action of air, they easily deteriorate, in spite of the generally practised compression; the essential oil which they contain becomes rancid and engenders a mouldiness, so that they do not keep longer than a year. To overcome this difficulty, and in order to give a more presentable aspect to his merchandise, the hop merchant has recourse to sulphuring, an operation always successful, but which at the same time produces a pernicious reaction on the essential oil, which thereby undergoes a chemical conversion. Under the action of the sulphurous acid, which passes over the hops, the essential oil is oxidized, converted into valerianic acid, and combines with the sulphur to form a solid body. In this manner the oily matter of the hops is destroyed and the mouldiness prevented; but beer manufactured with sulphured hops will never be a wholesome beverage. The aroma of the hops is replaced by that of the valerianic acid, the sulphurous acid contained in the hops is partly converted into sulphuric acid, and the sulphur of commerce being arseniferous, the arsenious acid passes with the sulphurous acid in the hops, both are communicated to the beer, and may, although taken in small doses, inconvenience the consumer.

Another disadvantage is the action of the sulphurous acid on the tannic acid in converting it into gallic acid, which prevents the clarification and the fermentation of the beers, besides giving them a rough or sour flavour. The due preservation of hops with all their active and useful properties, without being subjected to sulphurous fumigation, has been the object of long researches.

Ten years ago a soft and dry extract of hops was manufactured, containing in a small volume the bitter, tonic, and aromatic principles of the plant, of which it represented very nearly the fifth. This soft extract is a kind of brownish preserve, which, as it will not keep long, the brewer does not care to utilize; the dry extract which is still manufactured is in a coarse powder, and keeps better; it is used to improve the bitterness of beers in course of manufacture when they are too sweet.

The question that has occupied so much time has at last been solved: the preservation of hops without sulphuring and without the extraction of their bitter and tannic principles. By chemical and mechanical means the green or freshly dried hops are separated from their essential oil, the great obstacle to their preservation, so that the strobiles remain whole, keep their original colour, the yellow dust at the base of the scales, and all their bitter and tonic principles, the aroma excepted. Hops thus treated and compressed will, it is said, keep for years.

The essential oil is preserved by itself in hermetically sealed bottles, and improves from year to year.

In the manufacture of beer, one operates with these hops as usual; and after the fermentation ten or twelve drops of essential oil are added per hectolitre (22 gallons); the extraction of the bitter principle and of the tannin, the clarification and the fermentation are effected perfectly, the beer is of superior quality, very thin, limpid, clear, and creamy, being characterized by a delicious bouquet of hops, and keeps much better as, under the influence of the essential oil, the mycodemæ, microscopic animalculæ, which, by their presence in beer, cause an acetic and putrid fermentation, perish.

Chemistry of Hops.—Messrs. Payen and Chevallier, so far back as 1830, and even before, determined that the yellow secretion of hops, a bitter and aromatic element, was the sole source of the flavour, the strong odour, and, in fact, the active principle; and that the bracts of the cones which were not touched with the yellow substance, had no more aromatic odour or flavour than dry hay. They also ascertained that this yellow powder or secretion is found in varying proportions in different kinds of hops, and hence their real and useful value differs materially.

The following is the mode in which these able chemists made the analysis, which is more mechanical than chemical. "The strobiles, or cones, of the hops are taken when well dry, and the foreign matters which they contain are separated as much as possible; they are then placed on a fine horsehair sieve, pressed with the hand, and the sieve shaken; the pulverulent secretion passes through the meshes of the sieve, leaving the bracts on the top. These are again submitted to pressure and agitation, to separate any more of the yellow powder which may have escaped, until nothing is left but the waste bracts. Care, however, must be taken not to crush or bruise these, so that none may pass through the meshes to augment the bulk of the sifted powder. This product can then be weighed and preserved in closed vessels."

Dr. Ives found, on analysis, the lupulinic grains to contain

Tannin	4·16
Extractive	8·33
Bitter principle	9·16
Wax	10·00
Resin	30·00
Lignin	38·33
Loss	·02
	100·

The following analyses are useful for reference, as showing the percentage quality of the different hops of commerce, chiefly those of the Continent:

	Foreign Matters.	Waste Bracts.	Yellow Secretion.
Poperinghe (Belgium)	12·00	70·00	18·00
Old American	14·30	68·80	16·90
Bourges	0·50	83·50	16·00
Lake Crécy (Oise)	1·80	86·20	12·00
Bussignies	7·00	81·50	11·50
Vosges	3·00	86·00	11·00
Old English	3·00	87·00	10·00
Luneville	1·50	88·50	10·00
Liege	10·00	81·00	9·00
Alost	16·00	76·00	8·00
Spalt	3·00	88·00	8·00
Toul	1·50	91·50	8·00

Turpin recognized in the glands of the hops the presence of two vesicles in which an etherized oil existed, and Raspail, by a more careful examination, found chlorophyl, a resinous substance, an etherized oil, and some gluten in them. Payen and Chevallier analyzed hops from different sources, and they found as a minimum 8 per cent., and as a maximum 18 per cent. of hop dust. It is a well-known fact that the hops of different countries are not equally good; the difference in the quantity of the yellow powder may, among others, be one of the causes; but, as in the manipulations which the hops undergo, the yellow powder may be easily detached, it would be wrong to conclude from the experiments of Payen and Chevallier, that, in the hops as they are in the field, there exists such a difference in the quantity of powder; during the carriage a small quantity may in some way or other be lost.

Wimmer found in 100 parts of hops 20 parts of powder to 80 parts of scales. But as it was impossible to separate from the flowers all the particles of yellow dust held, he was of opinion that about half more ought to be added. He found, by analysis, the following percentages:

	Folioles of the Flower.	Yellow Dust.	Folioles and Dust together.
Volatile oil	..	0·12	0·12
Tannic acid	1·6	0·7	2·3
Bitter substance	4·7	3·0	7·7
Gummy ,,	5·8	1·3	7·1
Resinous ,,	2·0	2·9	4·9
Vegetable cells	64·0	9·0	73·0
	78·1	17·02	95·12
Watery extract	12·1	4·9	17·

Lupuline.—This name has been given by Ives to the yellow dust which covers the folioles of the female flower of hops. Later on Ives, Payen, Chevallier, and Pelletan gave the same name to the bitter substance contained in the dust.

Besides the oil which is obtained by distillation, and the tannic acid, which is also not without value as regards the preparation of beer, the resin and the bitter substance especially deserve to be distinguished. They are both obtained by treating with alcohol the yellow dust of the hops. Water is added to this tincture, and it is distilled, which causes the separation of a large quantity of resin. The tannic acid and malic acid are saturated by means of lime, and the liquor is evaporated. If the residue is treated by ether to further obtain a small remaining quantity of resin, then by alcohol, the bitter substance dissolves in the alcohol, and may be separated from it by evaporation.

Lupuline, seen under the miscroscope, resembles an acorn in its cupule; it is a gland composed of a hidden cupule, surrounded by a membraneous sac, called the *cuticule*, which contains the products of the secretion, constituting the essential oil of hops.

This essential oil is a clear green liquid, slightly bitter, very aromatic, of the mellow odour of fresh hops; its specific weight $= 908$ at $+ 16°$ C.; it is but slightly soluble in water, very soluble in alcohol, and boils at $+ 240°$ C. Iodine and bromine turn it brown and alcoholized sulphuric acid reddens it. The essential oil is composed of an eleoptine and a stearoptine. The eleoptine is a hydrocarbon, $C^{10}H^8$, isometric with spirits of turpentine, and distils at $+ 175°$ C. The stearoptine is an oxygenized hydrocarbon $C^{10}H^{12}O^2$, isomeric with valerol, which distils at $+ 210°$ C., and is converted by oxidation into valerianic acid.

The chemical composition of lupuline proves the richness of its principles, for analysis has found in it the following:

1. Water.
2. Essential oil.
3. Acetate of ammonia.
4. Malate of lime.
5. Albumine.
6. Gum.
7. Malic acid.
8. Tannic acid.
9. A resin.
10. Bitter extract.
11. A fatty matter.
12. Chlorophyl.
13. Acetate of lime.
14. Nitrate and sulphate of potash.
15. Sub-carbonate of potash.
16. Carbonate and phosphate of lime.
17. Phosphate of magnesia.
18. Sulphur.
19. Oxide of iron.
20. Silica.

In therapeutics, lupuline plays an important part, but the properties of the etherized narcotic extract, and those of a crystalline acid, in very bitter silky needles, which might be called humulin, have never been experimented on, and would probably be found powerful substitutes for opium and quinine.

The *bitter substance of hops* is a yellow solid matter, not very soluble in water, easily soluble in alcohol, less soluble in ether; it is odourless and of a very bitter flavour; has a feeble tendency to combine as easily with the metallic bases as with the acids. The *resin of hops* may be obtained pure by the action of boiling water. In the pure state this resin is free from all bitter flavour, it is insoluble in water; but is, on the contrary, very soluble in alcohol and in ether. The resin of hops has been the object of research by Vlaanderen. He treated the hop dust with boiling alcohol, then filtered it, added a considerable quantity of water, and evaporated it. In the yellow, cloudy liquor a soft resin of a dark brown colour is thrown down; this is separated from the liquor, again dissolved in alcohol, filtered, once more mixed with a large quantity of water, and evaporated, for the purpose of separating as much as possible by this evaporation the oil which remains adhering to the resin. The same treatment is recommended several times, and continued until the resin has lost all trace of bitterness.

The *etherized oil of hops* is a yellow oil, obtained, it is said, in the proportion of 2 per cent. from hop dust by distillation. I have, however, never seen it obtained in such a quantity. The resin retains moreover a very large quantity of oil. This volatile oil is more or less soluble in water, it easily dissolves in alcohol and in ether. Its specific weight has been found $= 0 \cdot 908$.

Way and Ogston on the one hand, and Hawkhurst on the other, have determined by analysis the constituent inorganic parts of hops. Watts and Nesbit have also effected the determination of them.

The following are their respective analyses:

	Way and Ogston.	Hawkhurst.	Nesbit.
Potass	12	25	19·4	25·2
Chloride of potassium	5			1·7
„ sodium		3		7·2
Lime	18	22	14·2	16·0
Magnesia	6	5	5·3	5·8
Sesqui-oxide of iron	2	2	2·7	7·5
				Phosphate of Sesqui-oxide of Iron.
Phosphoric acid	21	14	14·6	9·8
Sulphuric „	7	7	8·3	5·4
Silicic „	23	20	17·9	21·5
Carbonic „	5	2	11·0	
Soda			0·7	
Alumina			1·2	
Chlorine			2·3	
Amount of ash per cent.	8	6		

It is chiefly to its bitter principle that the physiological action which hops exert is generally due; this action has been compared to that of opium, and a narcotic power is generally attributed to hops, but I do not find sufficient reasons for this assertion.

In 1863 Lermer suggested the presence of a peculiar alkaloid in hops. Griessmayer's recent experiments seem to prove the existence of a peculiar volatile alkaloid, which he named lupilina. The concentrated aqueous decoction of ten pounds of hops was distilled with potassa or with magnesia, the distillate neutralized with muriatic acid, evaporated to dryness, treated with cold absolute alcohol, to remove sal-ammoniac, the alcoholic liquid heated to boiling, and evolved, when much muriate of trimethylamina crystallized. The filtrate evaporated in a water-bath, and finally spontaneously, the residue redissolved in water, in a narrow cylinder, agitated with potassa and ether, and the ethereal solution evaporated spontaneously. The remaining alkaline liquid had a peculiar odour, reminding of conia, and a cooling but not bitter taste. It soon separated in small crystals, and finally solidified completely. Other experiments proved that some kinds of hops contain no trimethylamina, and finally, also, that the substances present in hops go into beer.

CHAPTER II.

MEDICINAL USES OF HOPS.

Hops are used medicinally for their stomachic and tonic properties. They are also to some extent suporific, especially the odorous vapours from them; hence a pillow stuffed with hops is occasionally employed as an agreeable sedative to induce sleep, and was obtained for George III. when a lunatic. The extract has been found to allay pain; but after all, it is a better adjunct to beer than as a medicine. The infusion and tincture act as pleasant aromatic tonics, but Pereira doubts the existence of the narcotic effects which have been ascribed to hops.

He, however, states that the medicinal properties of hops are numerous. Both infusion and tincture of hops are mild and agreeable aromatic tonics. They sometimes manifest diuretic, or when the skin is kept warm, sudorific qualities. Their sedative, soporific, and anodyne properties are, however, very uncertain. Hops have been given internally to relieve restlessness consequent upon exhaustion or fatigue, to induce sleep in the wakefulness of mania and other maladies; to calm nervous irritation, and to relieve pain in gout and rheumatism. They have also been applied topically in the form of a fomentation or poultice, as a resolvent or discutient in painful swellings or tumours.

As the narcotic properties are due to the volatile oil, hops should be obtained as fresh as possible; and the medicinal tincture made from a fresh, well-matured hop is preferable to one made from old lupuline, although it would not be as uniform in strength, from the great range in quality; but as it is difficult to obtain either hops or lupuline fresh at all times, the lupuline is preferable, as it is of more uniform strength, and retains its properties longer. The hop, when old, is of very unequal strength, from the loss of lupuline sifted out in handling. For pharmaceutical use hops are pressed into quarter-pound, half-pound, and pound packages.

It is somewhat remarkable that lupuline has not found a place in the new Pharmacopœia of this country. It may, however, be said that it is not altogether ignored, inasmuch as it is extracted for that purpose, but the amount of it in different samples varies considerably, and it is certain that this peculiar powdery matter represents the active principles of the entire strobili in a concentrated form.

In order to free lupuline from sand, which often contaminates it, Sarrazin proposes to wash it with water. The lupuline was several times suspended in 10 parts of water, and poured off rapidly. It was then collected on a filter, and dried on it, at between 77° and 86° Fahr. From 5 grams he obtained 34 grains of purified lupuline, and the washings only contained between 2 and 3 grains of extract. The medicinal effect of the lupuline was not affected by the washing. Sarrazin[*] also proposes a liquid extract prepared as follows:

<small>Thirty parts lupuline are macerated in 100 parts alcohol for two days, filtered, the residue washed with a little more alcohol, and then infused in</small>

---

[*] 'Arch. Phar.,' Oct. 1874, p. 333.

200 parts water, strained, and evaporated on a steambath, the alcoholic extract being in the meantime evaporated at a temperature between 68° and 77° Fahr. The properly concentrated liquids are mixed and brought to the measure of 45 parts. The preparation, which is effective, requires shaking before dispensing it.*

Dr. Dyce Duckworth, in a communication to the 'Pharmaceutical Journal,' in 1868,† remarks:

"It is always desirable to possess the most powerful and concentrated preparation of the vegetable Materia Medica, and as no available active principle has as yet been separated from the hop, it should, in the meantime, be the endeavour of the pharmaceutist to obtain, and the physician to employ, the drug in its most complete and essential form. Hence I believe that at least one preparation of lupuline should be in use.

"The powder itself is inconvenient—from seven to twelve grains are requisite for a dose, and it must be given in the form of pill. In this way, too, an amount of lignin and other inert principles are ingested, which it is not desirable to employ, and which, in certain cases of gastric disease, would be positively harmful.

"This substance appears to be most fully appreciated in the United States of America. In the authorized codex of that country, I find there are no fewer than three preparations of it: a tincture, prepared with rectified spirit; a liquid extract (corresponding in strength to those of the 'Pharmacopœia Britannica,' viz. part for part); and an oleo-resin. The French Codex takes no notice of it. In the Edinburgh

---

* 'Arch. Phar.,' Oct. 1875, p. 331.
† Vol. x., Second Series, p. 246.

Pharmacopœia, there was a tincture made with rectified spirit; and lupuline was officinal in the Dublin Pharmacopœia.

"During a recent series of pharmaceutical experiments with the powder, I was constantly struck with the remarkable valerian-like odour evolved from the different preparations, and I was much interested to find, in the course of subsequent reading on the subject, that M. Personne had discovered valerianic acid in lupuline.*

"In none of the British Pharmacopœia preparations of hops, except the extract, can it be said that the real strength of the drug is removed. The tincture made with proof spirit, which does not thoroughly exhaust the active parts of the scales of lupuline, and the watery infusion can but inadequately represent the virtues of this medicine.

"The extract of hops, as prepared partly with spirit like the extract of jalap, has the advantage of containing some resin and volatile oil. It is the presence in so considerable an amount of resin, gum, and wax, in lupuline, that renders it important to select a proper solvent, and therefore proof spirit and water respectively are incapable of acting thoroughly upon it. We may, indeed, practically regard lupuline as a gum-resin, and to treat it pharmaceutically with success, we must apply the same solvents as we do in the case of drugs of that class. I have devised a preparation, which I think will prove most useful whenever it is desired to use the hop. It is an ammoniated tincture, and should be made in the same way as the other ammoniated tinctures of the Pharmacopœia.

"Like valerian, which also contains an oil and a resin,

* 'Comptes Rendus,' 1854.

lupuline is best exhausted by the aromatic spirit of ammonia, and the reason for this appears to be that this preparation contains the combination of alkali and rectified spirit necessary to the solution of the various elements in these drugs. Certainly no agent that I have tried extracts the virtues of lupuline so well as sal-volatile. The result is a strong, richly-coloured tincture. Neither rectified spirit, ether, nor of course proof spirit, produces so strong a preparation. I recommend the following formula :

"Lupuline, 2 oz.; spirit ammon. arom., a pint. Macerate for seven days, agitating occasionally; then filter and add sufficient of the menstruum to make up to a pint. The dose of this is from m. 20 to fl. ʒj.

"I have no hesitation in directing attention to this preparation of the hop as the best we at present possess. According to Christison, the dose of tinctura lupuli should be fl. ʒj to fl. ʒiss, to produce any hypnotic effect; the ordinary dose consists of as many drachms. Dr. Ives, of New York, states that the tincture of lupuline is an effectual hypnotic in restlessness, the result of nervous irritability, and in delirium tremens.* Some advantage, too, is derived from the presence of ammonia in considerable quantity, and this whether the preparation be exhibited as a hypnotic, or as a tonic combination of bitter and ammonia."

Mr. C. Lewis Diehl thus prepares the elixirs prescribed by the physicians of Louisville :

Elixir of Hops.— Add 2½ fluid ounces of fluid extract of hops—made according to the formula for fluid extract of gentian of United States —to 13½ fluid ounces of simple elixir; mix and filter.

---

* *Vide* American Codex, also Nevin's 'Translation of Lond. Pharm.,' 1851.

Elixir of Lupuline.—Triturate 2 ounces of fluid extract of lupuline with two ounces of carbonate of magnesia, add 14 fluid ounces of simple elixir, transfer to a bottle, agitate occasionally for several hours, and filter.

Extract of Hops.—In 1872, Professor C. A. Seeley, of New York, patented in the United States and England an improved process for extracting the useful substances of hops, and for manufacturing a pure and concentrated extract of hops. The invention is based on the discovery that the ordinary petroleum oils are rapid and complete solvents of the essential oils and of the bitter matter of hops. At the same time they have no solvent action on the other constituents of the plant, which in practical operations are either useless or hurtful. The improved process consists in steeping the hops in petroleum oil, and then by heat, stirring, digestion, and percolation, promoting the solvent action of the oil. When the extractable matter of the hops has been thus dissolved, the solution of hop extract in oil is separated by filtration from the refuse matter, and the solvent is volatilized or distilled off by heat; the extract thus being obtained free from the solvent and other foreign matter.

The kinds of petroleum oil proper for this purpose are naphtha and gasoline, which are the lighter and more volatile parts of crude Pennsylvania petroleum. Although any petroleum oil which has a boiling point below 212° Fahr. may be used, a gasoline which boils at about 100° Fahr. is preferable, because at that temperature the essential oil of hops will not escape from the extract solution when distilling the solvent.

The apparatus employed in manufacturing the solution and distilling the solvent is such as is suitable and well known for use where bisulphide of carbon, ether, hydrocarbons, or alcohol is used for analogous purposes. The extract of hops prepared as I have described is of a pasty consistency, more or less thin in proportion to the essential oil contained in it.

It is soluble in water, but slowly and only in small quantity. In order to increase its solubility in water, and to give it a more convenient consistency for measuring and transferring, sufficient alcohol is added to give it the consistency of thin syrup. This is probably the best form for a commercial extract of hops. This hop extract differs in some important respects from the extracts of hops hitherto known, and is therefore a new commercial product. It contains all the matter of the hop plant which it is desirable to use in the preparation of beer; while the saline and albumenoid substances found in alcoholic and watery extracts are wholly absent from it. The extract in its simple form is solid when cold, pasty when warm, and quite fluid at the boiling point of water."

Mr. Emmet Kannal, in the 'American Journal of Pharmacy,' gives the following recipe to prepare glycerole of lupuline:

"Take of lupuline 1 troy ounce, alcohol 6 fluid ounces, glycerine 9 fluid ounces, Curaçoa cordial 1 fluid ounce.

"Mix the alcohol with 2 fluid ounces of glycerine, moisten the lupuline with the mixture, pack it into a cylindrical percolator, and continue to add this mixture until 8 fluid ounces of the percolate has passed; to this add the remainder of glycerine, previously mixed with the Curaçoa, and thoroughly mix the whole together. This will afford by careful manipulation a very fine preparation miscible with any of the ordinary syrups or tinctures, and possessing all the medicinal properties of lupuline.

"Dose for an adult one teaspoonful, representing $7\frac{1}{2}$ grains of lupuline."

According to Wagner ('Chemical Technology'), the essential oil, the flavouring principle of the hops, is met with in air-dried hops, to the amount of 0·8 per cent.; it is yellow-coloured, with an acrid taste, without narcotic effect, of a specific gravity = 0·908, turning litmus paper red. It requires more than 600 times its weight of water to effect a solution. It is free from sulphur, and belongs to the group of essential oils characterized by the formula C_5H_8, and can become oxidized under contact with the air into valerianic acid ($C_5H_{10}O_2$), this oxidation being the cause of the peculiar cheesy odour of old hops; it is a mixture of a hydrocarbon C_5H_8 isomeric with the oils of turpentine and rosemary, with an oil containing oxygen $C_{10}H_{16}O$, having the property of oxidation alluded to.

Tannic acid is found in the several kinds of hops, in quantities varying from two to three per cent., and is an important constituent, as it precipitates the albuminous matter of the barley, and serves to clear the liquor. It gives with the persalts of iron a green precipitate; treated with acids and synaptase, does not separate into gallic acid and sugar; and by dry distillation, does not give any pyrogallic acid. The hop resin is the important constituent of the hops, and contains the bitter principle or lupuline. It is difficultly soluble in water, especially in pure water, and when the lupuline or essential oil is absent. But water containing tannic acid, gums, and sugar dissolves a considerable quantity of the resin, especially when the essential oil is present. It is intensely bitter in taste, and becomes foliated when exposed to the atmosphere.

Hop resin and the essential oil are not identical; the former is soluble in ether, the latter is not. In the course of long exposure it becomes insoluble. The gum and extractive colouring matter are of little use. The mineral constituents of hops dried at 100° are: ash, 9 to 10 per cent.; 15 per cent. of phosphoric acid; 17 per cent. of potash, &c.

Hops have recently been found to be a photo preservative. Numerous experiments having been made in the emulsion process, the desideratum has been found in ordinary hops—preferably the variety known as Bavarian, which seems stronger in certain qualities than the English hop. According to the 'British Journal of Photography':

"Two ounces of hops are infused for one hour in 20 ounces of water at a temperature of 170° Fahr., and the whole then turned into a cloth, and the liquid pressed out. When cold, 20 grains of pyrogallic acid and the albumen of two eggs are added, and the mixture is well shaken for ten minutes. It is then filtered into a dish and used in the ordinary way; or, if only a few plates are to be prepared, a smaller quantity may be made, and poured off and on several times. Plates preserved with this solution dry perfectly hard, have a fine gloss, and yield negatives of very high quality. The colour is a rich greenish-brown, and so non-actinic that over-development must be carefully guarded against. Although the solution can be easily made, it is desirable that, if possible, it should be made to keep, and therefore we have added carbolic acid and salicylic acid to separate quantities, and shall note the result on a future occasion.

"Meantime we consider the hop preservative, as above

indicated, a decided improvement on the beer and albumen. It possesses all its good, without any of its bad, qualities; the principal of which are the stickiness already referred to, the varying qualities of beer in different localities, and, especially, the irregular proportions of chlorides which, more or less, are always present, and to get rid of which many workers are in the habit of adding silver nitrate, which always introduces an additional element of uncertainty."

CHAPTER III.

SYSTEMS OF CULTIVATION.

THE culture of the hop involves a larger outlay than perhaps that of any of our other crops, ranging from 35*l*. to 60*l*. per acre. The returns from it are exceedingly variable, owing to the extreme liability of the plant to suffer from disease, and range from a little over 1 cwt. to 13 cwt. per acre; but unlike other crops known to our farmers, the duration of a plantation is almost indefinite, usually lasting, according to the situation and kind of treatment, from two to twenty years; indeed, some of the hop gardens at Farnham have not been changed for a new stock of plants since the introduction of hop culture into England more than 330 years ago.

The great value of the hop under favourable circumstances illustrates more forcibly the value of what is termed high farming than any other of our cultivated crops, and although its entire tillage and management are exceptional, yet from the examination of hop culture, as practised in some parts of the south of England, the agriculturist may derive many suggestive hints worthy of being acted upon in his ordinary operations. The outlay there in tillage, in manures, and in saving the crop is so large as almost to appear fabulous to those unacquainted with the details of management; but the enterprising and successful hop grower is aware that it is only by a liberal outlay (of course judiciously) that he can calculate on an adequate return.

The soil best adapted for the cultivation of the hop is a deep rich loam. In preparing the soil for this plant care should be taken to thoroughly destroy the weeds, and to reduce the soil to as pulverized a state as possible. Well-rotted dung must be applied with a liberal hand.

The plants or cuttings are prepared from old stools, and each should have two joints or eyes; from the one springs the root, and from the other the bine. They should be made from the healthiest and strongest bines, each being cut to the length of 5 or 6 inches.

The following is the best mode of planting: Strike furrows with the plough at equal distances of 8 feet; when finished repeat the process in the opposite direction. The hills are then to be made where the furrows cross each other, by digging out a spadeful of earth, and after mixing it with two spitsful of rotten dung, replacing the whole so as to form a small hillock; in this three or four plants are set at the distance of 5 or 6 inches from each other.

In dressing the hop plant, the operations of the first year are confined to twisting and removing the haulm. The former should be done about Christmas, by twisting the young vines into a knot so as to stop any further growth. The latter is performed with a sickle annually in the month of March; they should be cut even with the surface of the ground. The plants are generally ready for polling towards the end of September in the second and succeeding years. The poles should be from 16 to 20 feet long, the shoots should previously have risen 2 or 3 inches; three poles are generally set in each hillock; they should be planted at least 20 inches in the ground, and well secured, and they should not on any account lean toward each other. About the close of November the season for tying the bine commences. The most forward shoots should be extirpated, and the others tied to the pole. As the bines progress the persons employed to tie them will have to provide themselves with light ladders. This is all that will require to be done until the season for taking the crop. Hops are known to be ready for pulling when they acquire a strong scent, and the catkins become firm and of a brown colour. The bines are then cut even with the ground, the poles lowered carefully, and the hops picked off, after which they are dried in a kiln. This should be done as speedily as possible after they are picked, as if left for five or six hours they are apt to ferment and become unsaleable.

It is usual to plant one male to one hundred female sets; but one to one thousand might probably suffice. It requires good deep soil, as the plant roots deeply, and lasts a number of years.

Two or three sets should be put in together, and the earth heaped over them, these mounds being 6 feet apart every way. By having the mounds in one row opposite the spaces of the next, it enables you to run the plough, or horse hoe, in three directions, which is an advantage.

At this distance apart 1200 mounds will go to an acre; and as the average yield of each mound is about one bushel, or $1\frac{1}{2}$ lb., an acre will produce in a favourable season 16 to 18 cwt. of hops.

The first year poles of 6 feet are sufficient, but afterwards they will be required of 12 feet. No pruning is needed the first two years. After the second year the earth should be removed around the stump at the fall of the year, the old stem cut away, leaving two or three young shoots for the following year, and the mounds made up again over them.

Though from the yield per acre the profit would appear to be considerable, it must be borne in mind that hops are a very uncertain crop.

The expense of preparing the ground is large; trenching or double digging is in most cases indispensable, yet small patches of good earth may be found of several feet deep, in which case the labour would be saved.

The drying of the hop constitutes a very important part of its management; it is performed in kilns, generally of very unscientific construction, and apparently capable of great improvement. These are usually termed oasts or oast houses. The heat imparted by the fire in drying is of great importance, and should in no instance exceed 119° or 120° Fahr. The farina, or pollen, which falls through the hair-cloth or wire, in the course of desiccation, is a valuable article, and is denominated *hop dust*. If care is taken that no particles of fire fall into the kiln pit, and the hop dust be frequently removed therefrom, so as to ensure its freedom from extraneous matter, it is scarcely less useful to the brewer than hops themselves. One pound of the dust is equal to four times the quantity of the strobiles. In dark-coloured or common beer a small quantity might always be used without injury.

In order to give the hops a good colour, they are subjected to fumigation with sulphurous acid; after this process they are packed into sacks or pockets, and subjected to great pressure, so as to prevent access of air, and their consequent deterioration.

Mr. John P. Smith, of Worcester, has published in the 'Journal of the Royal Agricultural Society,' vol. xxv. p. 52, the following prize essay on the culture, which furnishes much useful information:

"The hop thrives best in moderately warm climates, and this may account for Kent and Sussex, two of the most southerly counties, being selected for its cultivation, and producing a very large proportion of the annual yield of the kingdom. Worcester and Hereford stand next in importance, and yield about one-eleventh of the yearly average growth. Farnham and its neighbourhood stand next as to quantity. The district known as the North Clays, in Nottinghamshire, formerly grew a fair quantity of good hops, but of late years the plantations have been much reduced; the same remark applies to the district around Stowmarket in Suffolk, and also to the county of Essex.

"A south-eastern aspect affords, in my opinion, the best situation for a hop garden, and if it be well protected from the west winds that prevail during the autumn, so much the better, as great mischief is often done by wind. Due care must be taken to adapt the planting to the peculiarities of the soil. The Golding hop will be found to succeed best on dry friable soil, with a gravelly or rocky subsoil, such as we find in the hilly districts of Middle and East Kent, while Mathon, White, and Grapes, prefer a stronger soil, approaching to clay; the former variety flourishes on the deep land in the vale of the Teme, and the latter in the Weald of Kent and

Sussex, which is mostly strong clay soil. Another variety, Cooper's White, a good sort, but delicate, is best suited for good strong loam. There are, besides, several kinds of red hops that are not approved by the brewer, and, in my opinion, cannot too soon become extinct; they are mostly grown on the poor lands of Herefordshire. Many other kinds are grown in Kent and Sussex, viz. Golden Tips, Pheasants, Golden Grapes, White bines, Grapes, Jones's, &c., and a sort introduced some few years since by Mr. Colegate, and known by his name. This is a hardy variety and heavy cropper, but subject to blight, and repudiated by the brewer as a rank bad hop, yielding a most unpleasant flavour to the beer. A young planter should avoid this if he wishes to obtain a good character for his growth.

"We will now assume that a suitable field—one that has been thoroughly drained—has been selected, and the preference given to an old piece of turf; in that case I would recommend that the land be trenched two spits deep, the top spit being kept uppermost, with the turf downwards. When the digging is finished, the surface should be harrowed, and rolled down as fine and level as possible, ready for setting out. The planter must next determine on the arrangement of the rows, whether on the angle or the square, and the distance from plant to plant. The usual method in Worcestershire and Herefordshire is to lay out the rows 7 or 8 feet apart, and set the plants $2\frac{1}{2}$ to 3 feet distant in the rows. If your land be good, and likely to be highly farmed, an uniform distance of 7 feet square may be recommended; good cultivation will ensure a large quantity of bine, and a sufficient quantity of sun to bring the fruit to perfection, whilst at this distance you have more room to cultivate without injuring the bines.

"If this plan is adopted, you must prepare 889 small sticks, a foot to 18 inches long, for every acre, that being the number of hills which an acre will take at 7 feet square. First square your field, and then commence in the centre, working right and left; you will thus be more likely to be correct than if you begin on one side.

"Your field being truly set out, you may prepare for planting; if you plant bedded or yearling sets (which are far preferable to cuttings), a man should take a spade, and remove the soil from two sides of the stick, the opening being 2 inches wide at the top, and 4 to 5 inches at the bottom, which should be deep enough to let the roots lie straight. Two strong-bedded roots are sufficient for a hill, but if not strong, three may be better. Care should be taken to bring the head of each root as close to the stick as possible; some good, fine soil should then be put to the roots, and made firm with the foot. For a plantation of 20 acres, with suitable oasts and cooling rooms to dry and cool the crop in one month, for a first-class growth, the following varieties are recommended: 5 acres of Cooper's White, or 3 Cooper's and 2 Jones's; 6 acres Mathon's; 6 or 7 acres of Goldings, and 2 or 3 acres of Grapes; but this distribution of sorts must, in a measure, be governed by the quality of the land, that variety being most largely planted which is best suited to the soil. The crop ought to be secured in three weeks, or certainly not more than a month; and it is most important to have an early sort, such as Cooper's White or Jones's, to commence with; then will follow your Mathons, then the Goldings, and lastly, the Grapes, a hardy sort, which will hang well for the last picking. Jones's are serviceable to use up old poles. The writer has seen a ton an acre on 7-feet poles. If, as is mostly the case in Sussex, one variety only be planted, you must begin to pick before your hops are ripe, or have a considerable proportion brown before you can finish.

"If the planter should determine on a piece of old tillage, I recommend him to plough 10 inches, and subsoil as deep as he can; the ploughing completed, he will proceed the same as if it had been a meadow, with this exception, that after the sticks are truly set, he should dig holes 2 feet in diameter, and 2 feet deep, placing the top or best soil on one side, and the bottom soil on the other side of the hole obliquely, so that the heaps may not interfere with replacing the sticks when the holes are refilled. Good dung, or rather a rich compost, should be wheeled on, and a fork or shovelful mixed with the best soil after the hole has been half filled with good soil from the surface; this being finished, you must readjust your sticks, and when your soil has had time to settle, you may proceed to plant in the manner before described. On no account bury your manure. Should the weather be favourable, and your roots get a start, they will require two poles to each hill 6 to 7 feet long, and if the season be good, a crop of 2 or 3 cwt. an acre may be grown; if cuttings are planted you lose a year.

"Potatoes and mangold are frequently planted between the rows, and an ox-cabbage between each hill; this will, by many, be condemned, but much depends on the condition of the land and the disposition of the planter to make compensation to the soil, for what has been taken out by the green crops, by a dressing of manure, which must be applied in the winter and dug in. Turnips may be planted if the land admits of their being fed off; and this plan, if oil-cake or corn be given, will manure the land at a cheap rate, greatly to the benefit of the hops.

"February and March are the months best suited for throwing down and cutting, the land being first ploughed or dug. If the plough is used, a slip from 12 to 15 inches wide is left. Your men will commence digging these slips, cleaning the hills, and cutting the roots: this finished, your poles must be spread, and your pile rows ploughed, dug, and cut the same as the rest.

"In the course of a fortnight or three weeks the bines will begin to appear, when no time should be lost in pitching the poles, which should be set by line to ensure regularity: the poles for this season, if the roots are strong, may be from 10 to 12 feet. The next operation is tying, but the tier should first go over and take out the rank hollow bines; these should, on no account, be put up the poles, since they have a tendency to grow to an extravagant quantity of bine, without bearing a proportionate quantity of fruit—the next and less vigorous bines will be found far more fruitful. Some planters put three bines up each pole: if four poles are put to a hill, which is the custom at 7 feet square, two bines will be found sufficient; if three poles, put two twos and a three. The writer has often seen a heavy produce from a single bine. The tiers are paid by the acre, and go over the hills three or four times until the poles are furnished, when all superfluous bines and weeds are pulled out. This completes the tying, except by ladder, which is paid for extra. The men now follow, dig round the hills, and put a shovelful of soil into each hill—this prevents new bines from springing up.

"Different varieties require different-sized poles. On no account over-pole, as much injury has resulted from it; 14-foot poles are long enough for any variety except Goldings, and for them I would not, as a rule, exceed 15 feet. Jones's will do well with 8 feet; Grapes 10 to 12, Cooper's 12, and Mathon's 12 to 14 feet, according to cultivation and quality of land. When your hops are tied, no time should be lost in working them with the nidget or scuffle, followed by the harrow—this should be done both ways. All workings should be finished by the 1st of July, certainly by the 10th; considerable mischief is often done by working too late, unless in years of blight. When you have vermin on your bines, do nothing to your land—leave them until the vermin disappear—then go in with all your strength, nidget both ways, and do all you can to put fresh vigour into the plant. Some planters manure in the winter, and some both winter and summer; but this may be carried too far for quality, and produce mould. The plan adopted in summer is to wheel in good dung or compost, take the soil from round the hills, put in the manure, and dig it in; or spread the compost (which I prefer) round the hills on the surface, and dig in. All that is necessary after is to use your nidget, and harrow both ways, taking care not to pull up the dung. This should complete the work, unless hoeing is required to keep down annuals.

"Picking commences in early seasons from the 1st to the 8th September; in late ones, from the 15th to the 20th. Before it begins due provision should be made, and everything got in readiness: cokes may be sent for in July and August, and a sufficient number of pickers engaged to keep your kilns or oasts properly at work. In this you must be governed by the size of the hops. Different plans are adopted in picking and measuring; some measure by tally, others by book and cards representing the number of each crib or bin. I have found it best to put two cribs into the centre of 100 hills; this is called a "house," and the cribs remain until the work is finished. The poles will be in two heaps at either end of the cribs, and in the proper place for stripping and piling. If this is strictly carried out, much trouble is saved in piling the poles. When a sufficient number of sacks are picked to load one kiln (and this should be done before breakfast), they should be taken and put on the oast, and so on until all your kilns or oasts are loaded; and it should be so managed that hops enough be picked to reload the kilns at night.

"Hop drying requires great attention, and the slower, in reason, they are dried, the better. They should be dried by a current of hot air being continuously passed through them, and not by combustion. Many say they can dry hops in seven or eight hours; rely on it, it is better to take twelve, and let your heat not exceed 112 to 115 degrees. When the hops are sufficiently dried, the fire should be raked or allowed to go down, the hops remaining on the kiln until they become soft, which will prevent their breaking on being removed to the cooling room. These hops will be fit to be bagged the next day, and with a proper staff this should be carried out through the picking.

"Poles are a heavy item in the cost of hop cultivation, and

should be properly husbanded. Their wearing value may be doubled by pickling 2½ feet at the sharpened end with creosote. A tank for the purpose must be erected of size in proportion to the plantation. By the application of creosote soft wood, such as that of the willow, &c., becomes hardened and equal to ash or other more durable sorts.

"The writer has a plantation of 75 acres, and a tank 12 feet long by 5 wide, and 3½ feet deep. This tank will hold 1000 best poles put to stand up. The tank must be filled with creosote within 8 inches of the top when the poles are in, when water fully 2 inches deep must be added to prevent evaporation. The tank should boil slowly twenty-four hours, when the poles may be removed and the tank refilled. Care must be taken that the tank does not boil over, as creosote is most inflammable, and may take fire. I am so satisfied as to the value of creosoting poles that I never intend to put a new pole into my ground without its aid. If poles were pickled one year under another, and stored in a stack till dry, they would be found to last far longer than if used in a green state.

"The hop plant has a variety of enemies: on the first appearance of the bine it is frequently attacked by flea, which checks its growth, and makes it look scrubby and unhealthy, but never destroys the crop. Wireworms are a great pest; the best plan to get rid of them is to cut a potato in half, and place it close on either side the root an inch below the surface; the potato lures the worm, and, if taken up every other morning for a fortnight, enables you to take a great quantity; I have known of a dozen being taken from one root. The greatest enemy is the aphis, and I regret to say that on the most important subject of its history we are as ignorant as our forefathers; we go to bed leaving our garden free, and next morning we find aphides—from one to ten or twenty—on a small leaf, which in the course of a week have increased to countless myriads. These pests are followed by nits and lice, which some seasons multiply so rapidly as to destroy the bine and the planter's prospects. I would here repeat the recommendation which I have already given to the planter, not to work his hops when in a state of blight. When closely watching the blights of 1860, '61, and '62, I have observed that in all cases where the land was best tilled, manured, and cared for, the blight remained until too late in the season for the chance of a crop; on the other hand, where nothing was done, but weeds were suffered to grow nearly half-way up the poles, the bine became yellow and clean, and the result was a fair sprinkling of hops; in such ground, the vermin had left the hop for want of sap and taken to the weeds.

"Of late years a machine has been used to pack the hops which is very useful when there is a large crop, as it enables you to pack your hops much sooner. Treading up is preferable, if care be taken to have the hops in a fit state not to break under the foot; if allowed to become too cool they are hard and lumpy in the sample, and are termed cold. A master's attention to the state of his hops before bagging is most necessary to good management. Hops are picked in Worcestershire and Herefordshire far more free from leaves than in Kent or Sussex. They should be sent, if possible, to the oast without a leaf, dried slowly, taken off the kiln in a soft, not a brittle state, and trod into the pocket as soon as sufficiently cool; they do not then break under the foot. In Kent and Sussex hops are dried in a variety of ways, and with several kinds of fuel. In oasts on the Cockle principle anything may be used, and a considerable quantity of sulphur is required; but on the open fire principle Welsh coal and coke is used, and a small quantity of sulphur.

"The cokes we get from Abberley and Pensax, in Worcestershire, are highly charged with sulphur, which will account for so little being added in these counties. Its only value is to give brilliancy to the sample, and, if used in excess, brewers object to it as affecting the fermentation of their worts.

"It has been the practice in Worcestershire and Herefordshire to make eight sacks out of one piece of cloth of 36 yards, and the weight of the pockets when filled runs from 1 cwt. 1 qr. to 1 cwt. 2 qrs. It is my practice to make seven sacks from a piece, and I am thereby enabled to get 1 cwt. 2 qrs. to 1 cwt. 3 qrs. into a pocket, and I would respectfully recommend my brother-planters to do the same. A heavy pocket has many advantages over a light one; you pay less for weighing, porterage, and warehouse rent, and you get your hops more quickly into consumption.

"It was formerly the practice to roll, riddle, and otherwise break and spoil good hops; this silly method is in a great measure exploded. Plant the best sorts, such as Coopers, Mathons, and Goldings; pick them clean, dry them properly, and put them into the pockets as whole as possible. By breaking the hop you lose a large quantity of the pollen, which contains the most valuable brewing properties.

"The cost of hop cultivation per acre may be estimated as follows:

	£	s.	d.
Yearly charge for poles	5	0	0
Ploughing down	0	10	0
Digging slips, or portion not ploughed	0	5	0
Cutting, picking up, and burying roots	0	4	0
Spreading poles	0	2	0
Pitching or setting poles	0	12	0
Tying	0	8	0
Nidgeting or scuffling 4 times	1	0	0
Harrowing 4 times	0	6	0
Forking round hills and hilling up	0	5	0
Stripping and piling poles	0	8	0
Resharpening broken poles	0	3	0
Ploughing up before winter	0	10	0
Manuring, if with dung, 20 loads per acre, at 8s.	8	0	0
If manured in summer	4	0	0
Ladder tying	0	2	0
	21	15	0
If you dig instead of plough, 15s. per acre extra	0	15	0
Total	£22	10	0"

CHAPTER IV.

CULTIVATION AND MANAGEMENT OF THE HOP—*(continued)*.

Mr. John Noakes, of the Furnace Farm, Lamberhurst, well known as one of the most successful hop-growers, read a paper recently before the Tunbridge Wells Farmers' Club "On the Cultivation and Management of Hops," from which I make the following extracts:

"The first step, and which I consider important, is to get the land as bare of herbage as possible, and to do this I would recommend crowding on a number of sheep, to be trough-fed, two or three weeks before the breaking up of the land. By so doing the turf is much easier buried, and the land is made solid and firm much sooner than when a quantity of old grass is ploughed in. I prefer to plough two furrows when the subsoil is loamy or broken than doing it in one operation. The first furrow I have very fleet—less than 3 inches if possible—the horses to walk in the furrow, on the sod when ploughing the second, which ought to be not less than from 8 to 9 inches, making in all nearly 12 inches, which is better than a greater depth. If the subsoil is clayey or retentive, it is better to plough one furrow only, from 9 to 10 inches deep, the horses of course walking on the surface. Arable land should be ploughed deeper than ordinary ploughing and subsoiled. For this purpose fine, dry weather should be chosen, in order that the horses may walk on the surface. The subsoiling may be done with the ordinary plough without the wrest plough, but Reed's subsoil plough is preferable. Sufficient care is not taken when planting hops, and it often occasions much delay. It is too frequently left until the busy season of digging and dressing, when the operation is hurried, and consequently often very badly done. About the middle of February, should the weather permit, is the best time for planting; the frost after that time is not so likely to draw the seeds as when planted in November (a time some prefer), and there is sufficient time for the soil to close well round the roots before the earth gets dry in the spring. Care should also be taken to provide a mixture of dung and mould to plant in, either on pasture or arable. The proper distance for planting will vary according to sort, soil, and situation. I prefer generally 6 feet 6 inches, but on uplands, rather exposed, where Jones's are intended to be planted and short poles used, 6 feet or 6 feet 3 inches is a preferable distance. Three poles to the hill, 6 feet 6 inches plant, which will give 3090 poles to the acre, will grow more hops, in my opinion, than 6 feet plant with two poles to the hill, 2420 to the acre. The wide plant also has its advantages in the expense of tying, cultivation, &c. I much prefer bedded to cut sets, either for pasture or arable land; they are more likely to form a strong hill sooner than cut. Two sets are sufficient for a hill, and are better than more, if they are strong and well rooted. Many planters cut nearly all the roots off—in fact, reduce them almost to a cut set. I do not approve of this plan; I much prefer to plant the set nearly as it is taken up, only tipping the coarse roots, and taking off those that are bruised. Neither is sufficient care taken generally to get sets true of their kind and from a distance. I would rather buy sets at a good price far from home than have those grown near given to me. It is no doubt equally as important as a change of corn for seed. Many planters grow turnips, mangold wurzel, or potatoes amongst their young hops, and I have seen cabbage and kohl rabi. I think it is wrong to do so, and the old maxim "penny wise and pound foolish" applies well to this practice. I consider anything of the kind I have mentioned planted amongst young hops, besides taking much out of the land, rather encourages grub, wireworm, &c., and hinders cultivation. It is much better to cultivate well, and set traps of slices of mangold wurzel to the hills to catch wireworm, &c., to have these constantly attended to, and so thoroughly destroy the vermin entrapped. On meadow land not well drained, I should advise its being done after the sticks are set, and previous to planting. On arable land it should be done in the autumn or winter, after the planting. It is most important that the land should be thoroughly and deeply drained. The greater portion of my hop land is drained 5 feet deep. Where the soil would not permit of that depth, it is 4 feet, and none less. I take it as a rule, land that will not bear deep drainage is not hop land at all. Since the introduction of ploughing, planters are more independent of casual labour, which was often bad in quality and expensive. Although I plough a little occasionally, and that only in fine weather, when the land will bear the horses, I much prefer digging. The saving by ploughing is very trifling, if any, when we consider the cost of digging, which, on an average, is about 20s. per acre. I think it wrong to dig young hops the first winter after planting, until after they are poled. I have seen considerable injury done by digging too closely to the hills, and many sets and even hills dug up entirely. It is best to get the poles stocked and the manure carted early on the young ground. At the beginning of March or before, if the weather is favourable, the dead bine should be cut off and the hill cleared of all weeds. About the third week in March the poling should commence, and the digging immediately follow. The dipping or creosoting of hop poles has caused a great change in our system of poling. Large 14-foot poles are no longer necessary, except in a very few instances. Moderate-sized well-cut 13-foot poles are found to be sufficient for Colegates and Goldings. Jones's, instead of taking the refuse from other grounds of very uneven length, varying from 7 feet to about 12 feet, are now poled with nearly the same degree of uniformity as other kinds. Greater care is now required in arranging the poles to the ground than formerly. It is now easy to over-pole, which I have seen frequently done, much to the injury of the planter; but under the old system the sharpening down would generally obviate that danger. Many growers dip their poles without being scraped. I do not approve of the plan, as the bark must hinder to a great extent the creosote entering the pole. It is very doubtful economy, as the cost for scraping—$3d.$ per hundred for small bundles, and $4d.$ for large—is very trifling. It is very important to have the poling done well; whether the work is well done or indifferently done, the difference is of considerable weight per acre. It is often the practice to crowd the poles too near the hill, in which case after they are put up they are in too slanting a direction, the tips of the poles get together as the weight of the bine and hops increase, to the injury of the crop and sample. Poles should be set firmly in the ground, nearly upright, and the width of plant and length of pole should regulate the distance apart at the bottom, so that the tops are an equal distance apart. It is clear by poling upon this plan every pole gets equal benefit from sun and air, which they do not when netted together and housed, as they frequently are. Dipping gives us the opportunity of early poling, which I consider a great advantage. Frost is not so likely to injure the young bines, and the best bines are not bruised and broken as they often are when poled late. All planted hops should have short poles to them: they root much stronger than if allowed to run the ground or twisted up, as was the practice formerly. The new modes of training hops I am not in favour of. The string system is being gradually discontinued, and Coley's inclined system (an improvement upon the string) I do not think will come into general use. I need not dwell upon the cultivation after poling, but simply remark I am not an advocate for deep nidgeting until after the first week in July; after that to nidget with one horse shallow, and frequently. I approve of the plan of striking and raking off before picking, because the land is firmer after picking, and resists the heavy rains of winter—in fact, is altogether in a better state than when autumn striking is resorted to. Manures should be put generally all over the ground, except in a few instances, such as weak plants, or when hops from some cause require an immediate stimulant. In that case rapedust or some kind of artificial manure may be chopped in round the hill to advantage, but I would not advise its being put too close. The last season has been a most anxious one for the growers—at one time threatened with almost total blight, then a ray of hope that we should grow a few. Those who resorted to syringing were equally dismayed. The blight was so tenacious that the operation was obliged to be repeated over and over again, without apparently any good effect. At last, however, perseverance was rewarded, and syringing prevailed. In the meantime, it will be remembered, great atmospheric changes took place—the wind veered from the east to south, and then to west. Favoured with warm showers, the hops, not washed even, and not irretrievably gone, responded in a marvellous and almost unprecedented manner. The district is certainly favoured, whether syringed or not; and growers can congratulate each other alike, and singularly enough, though we have experienced another blight, the advantages of syringing are much doubted and still remain subject for much discussion. It is a fortunate circumstance that those who syringed are satisfied, and those who did not are satisfied also. I can confidently tell anyone who may syringe in future that soft soap is all that is required, and that tobacco and other ingredients are an unnecessary expense. Mould is now very prevalent in the Weald of Kent, much worse than formerly, and it is to be attributed to various causes—firstly, to the introduction of new sorts; secondly, planting on land with too shallow soil, and using artificial manure almost entirely; and thirdly, planting kinds not adapted for the soil. The free use of sulphur is generally a remedy, but there are instances where it has had but little effect. My plan is to use about 50 lbs. of sulphur per acre on the first appearance of mould, and to continue at intervals of about a week until the bur is breaking into hops. By adopting this plan, I have never had mould to do me injury. Other forms of blight I am happily not acquainted with, excepting red' spider or rust, which I am not much troubled with. If I should have it to any extent I should use sulphur, as I understand, if taken in time, it is generally effectual. It is important so to arrange our plantations as to have a succession of sorts judiciously selected, and sufficient oast accommodation to enable us to secure the whole growth with colour and in good condition. More oast room is required now than formerly, when good ripe yellow and rather brown hops were esteemed, but now are very unsaleable. Too early picking is no doubt wrong, although occasionally we may get a coloury choice sample, but the loss in weight, injury to the stock, and other drawbacks are incalculable. The drying or management of hops is perhaps more important than any part of the cultivation. Formerly, very poor accommodation was given for drying. With the hair but a few feet from the fire, a very short rafter, with very little air admitted, the hops were baked rather than dried. Although great improvement has taken place during the last few years in the picking and management, more kiln room is generally required to secure the crop in the best possible condition, and also to prevent excessive overloading, so injurious to the sample and the great disadvantage of the grower. There is a great difference of opinion as to whether the old cockle principle or open fires are best. I am of opinion cockles are best suited to the Weald of Kent. Less skill is required in drying; they are more economical in fuel, and, if not superior, a softer and equally good sample may be produced, without the danger of scalding or burning which there is with the open fire. The plan I adopt, and which I think the best, is to load moderately, not to hurry the drying, but to keep the hops on the hair nearly twelve hours; not to turn them unless quite necessary, nor take them off before they are dried quite sufficiently, but lump them in the cooling room, well cover them with cloths, and allow them to remain until the next oasting is ready to come off. They are then uncovered, and, should there be any tough on the outside of the lump, they are raked off and put back on the kiln to come off with the next load. The lump is then removed for treading. I have pursued this plan for the last ten years, and during that time have not had a single pocket objected to or rejected on account of mismanagement. Some years— there being an exceedingly good growth, both for colour and quality—the presser has the advantage, but generally I am in favour of the old plan of treading."

In hop drying a good deal of difference still exists as to the comparative advantages of the round and the square kilns. The former is said to save much fuel; but whether round or square it should have an improved chimney, with plenty of length, and great draught at the bottom. So much, however, does not depend on the construction of this oast as on the merits of the hop dryer.

Formerly the dryers dried directly the hops were put in, and before the "reek" was gone off, and some of the old dryers do the same now. This custom caused the lower stratum of hops in the kiln to bake together, and the steam discoloured the upper portion. With a better mode of drying, a much better sample might be obtained with a slight alteration of the old kilns. What is required is, that the fire should not be too brisk; it could not be too slow till the "reek" is gone off, and after that the hops could not well be hurt. The great thing is to get a good draught. Nothing is gained by lighting up the fire so early as is done by some of the old dryers, as the hops being caked up in a mass by the steam, could not be dried any the sooner for it. Probably in nine out of ten of the old oasts the "reek" could not get away.

The following estimate of the cost of raising and cultivating an acre of hops is given by Mr. John Buckland, the author of the Royal Agricultural Society's prize essay on the Farming of Kent; and, with some exceptions, it is a very close approximation to the truth; indeed, in Mid Kent even higher expenses have been incurred in forming and cultivating hop plantations.

1.—Raising the Plantation.

	£	s.	d.
Ploughing and subsoiling	1	10	0
Harrowing	0	5	0
50 loads manure at 2s.	5	0	0
Setting out hills	0	2	6
Digging holes, and filling with manure	1	5	0
5000 plants at 6d. per 100	1	5	0
Planting	0	8	0
Expenses of planting	9	15	6
Horse-hoeing, 5 times	1	5	0
4-foot poles, 1 to each hill, and labour	0	5	0
Chopping round the hills	0	6	8
Striking furrows, &c.	0	3	4
Draining, 240 rods at 9d.	9	0	0
Rent, taxes, and tithe	2	0	0
Total cost, first year	£22	15	6

It should be remarked that in Mid Kent the large item of 9*l.* per acre for draining is not incurred, the subsoil being naturally porous and open, so that no draining is necessary; and even on the heavier soils so large an outlay as 9*l.* per acre is not necessary to effect the most complete drainage, except, perhaps, in places where, from the flatness of the land, no good outfall for the drains can be obtained. There, in order to make an effective drainage by means of shallow drains, they must be more frequent, and consequently the expense will be greater. Neither, where draining is needed, ought it to be charged specifically to the hops, for all the land ought to be alike drained, whether used for hop growing or ordinary farming. Practically, on the heavier lands of Kent, draining is often confined to the hop plantations, and thus it does with a great many of the Kentish farmers, in fact, form a specific expense of the hop plantation.

2.—Cost of Cultivating from the Second to the Sixth Year, both inclusive.

	£	s.	d.
Striking up and furrowing	0	5	0
Stripping and stacking poles	0	6	6
Digging, at 21*d.* per 100	0	17	6
Manure and carting on	8	0	0
Pruning, at 6*d.* per 100	0	5	0
Sharpening poles and poling, at 1*s.* 6*d.* per 100	0	15	0
Tying, at 10*d.* per 100	0	8	4
Ladder tying	0	3	0
Chopping, at 9*d.* per 100	0	7	6
Horse-hoeing 5 times, rolling, &c.	1	5	0
Hilling, at 3*d.* per 100	0	2	6
Setting up poles, &c.	0	3	0
Poles and carting	8	10	0
Rent, and repairs to oast	1	5	0
Rent, rates, and tithes	2	10	0
Interest on capital, 30*l.* per acre	1	10	0
Cost of cultivation per annum	£26	13	4

	£	s.	d.
Brought forward	26	13	4
Estimated growth, 10 cwt. per acre per annum:			
Picking	5	0	0
Drying, packing, &c.	3	10	0
Duty	8	14	6
Total cost per annum	£43	17	10

An entire plantation would not perhaps cost quite so much, but the estimate is given, and seems to be pretty generally accepted, as a "fair average." This estimate is framed on a Weald of Kent plantation, and the cost of a plantation in Mid Kent is confessedly higher, but then the Mid Kent hops bring higher prices than those grown in the Weald. The first year produces no crop, and that of the second is very trifling, so that an idea of the hazard incurred in hop growing looks rather startling. As a measure of the precariousness of the culture, I give, on the same authority, a summary of the produce and money receipts of a hop plantation in the Weald of Kent for ten years, from 1835 to 1844; during which time the price of the hops sold ranged between 48s. and 150s. per cwt.

Years.	Acres.	Growth.	Sold for.	Average per Acre.
		cwts.	£	cwts.
1835	27½	315	1148	11
1836	30	245	801	8
1837	28	207	727	7
1838	25¼	298	1202	11
1839	21½	329	939	15
1840	22⅔	14	79	0
1841	22¼	223	1316	9
1842	22¼	228	962	10
1843	25¼	274	1523	10
1844	25½	78	549	3

CHAPTER V.

QUALITY AND KEEPING OF HOPS. STATISTICS OF CULTURE
AND PRODUCTION IN ENGLAND.

THE following extract from Tizard gives an opinion on some of the varieties of hops:

"Farnhams," he states, "are in high repute, though not worth the price the brewer usually gives for them, unless the proximity of his residence be a consideration in their favour. The North Clays are rankest in taste, and fetch a better price with a certain class of buyers than those from Kent, though not generally so high as the Farnham variety. Those grown in the neighbourhood of Canterbury have been much prized for their superiority, but that is not invariable. The produce of the county of Kent, though pre-eminent both for strength and flavour, differs according to soil and season, which are not always adapted to each other. The Wealds are celebrated in some of the southern and midland counties, but in those more north, as Cheshire and Lancashire, the Worcesters are preferred for their mildness, and for the grateful sensation they yield; some use a few Sussex or Kents with them, but most brewers in the counties just referred to reject the growth of Kent as unpleasing to their customers.

"But however good the produce of any district may be in general, it must not be supposed that there are no bad samples of those varieties. Such bags should be chosen as are heaviest, because it is the farina which gives weight, and hops which lose a part of it from fine weather or over ripeness in picking or turning on the oast, will considerably diminish in gravity.

"They should feel clammy when handled, should be uniform in colour, without greenish particles in the flower, and full of hard seeds, and farina or condition. Mould may be discovered in the sample by the strig of the flower being partly bare of leaf. Particular attention must also be paid to crust, proceeding from damp or bad keeping, as it injures the quality more than age.

"New hops, like new teas, have a larger proportion of volatile oil than old hops, and there is a strife amongst the growers to bring the earliest supply to the market."

English hops, well prepared and especially well packed, soon acquired a high and merited reputation; then Germany and Austria began to give increased attention to the cultivation and preparation of hops, and selected fine and delicate species. There are several varieties distinguished on the Continent, such as common hops, those in which the cones are formed of large and thick bracts, at the base of which are found small resiniferous yellow grains of an aromatic and bitter flavour. The Flanders hops have also large cones, thick with short dense bracts and dry lupuline. The English hops are strong, of a rough flavour, the bracts and cones large. The German hops have the delicate bracts on the cones, of the colour of Sienna earth; the lupuline grains are small, transparent, and oily to the touch, adhering to the fingers.

It is highly necessary that brewers should have determined for them the quality of the hops they employ, because according to the quantity of aromatic matter which they contain will the useful principles to be extracted be found more or less active. It is not, however, alone this bitter principle which is useful in brewing, because we find among the components of the hop, tannin, a colouring matter, gum, resin, &c., each of which elements has some effect upon the beer. Thus an analysis of hops shows the following:

Water	14·50
Aromatic oil	0·50
Resin	15·90
Tannin	3·02
Gum	11·10
Colouring matter	6·40
Cellulose	48·30
Salts	0·28
	100·00

At the London Exhibition of 1862 this important product was represented by samples from every hop-producing district of England, from two British colonies, from twelve European countries, and from the Northern States of America. The jury in their Report stated, that in regard to delicacy of flavour, brightness of colour, and perfection of curing, English hops maintain their well-merited high reputation. In strength or amount of lupuline the hops from Bavaria and Bohemia can hardly be surpassed, while, for the most part, their curing was excellent.

The samples from other German states (often represented as Bavarian) are generally of fair moderate strength and flavour, but too often badly cured, and packed with too many green leaves.

France exhibited hops from Alsace and Lorraine, of excellent flavour, but somewhat deficient in strength. They were carefully picked, and in some cases very well cured.

From Belgium most of the samples exhibited the usual fault of hops from that kingdom, being badly picked, with too much stalk and green leaves, and with a smell of smoke from bad curing.

The hops from Canada and the United States still exhibit the disagreeable flavour which renders them quite unsuitable for fine qualities of ales.

Hops were also shown from the Netherlands, Denmark, and Greece, but of very inferior quality.

Portugal exhibited samples of wild hops, which seem to indicate the possibility of successful cultivation there.

The hops must on no account be gathered until the seed is perfectly ripe, as it is only then that the bitter quality is fully developed. The ripeness of the hops can be ascertained by rubbing them between the fingers; if an oily matter remains, with a strong odour, they are fit for gathering.

The aroma, which is very agreeable, is extremely volatile, and hence the necessity for closely packing the hops, as is done in practice when they are to be preserved. Under any circumstances, however, much of the aroma of the hops will be lost by keeping, a circumstance rendering it indispensable that they should be used as fresh as possible, especially in the manufacture of superior descriptions of ale and beer.

Preservation of Hops.—The hop plant cannot, like grain, be preserved for an indefinitely prolonged time without undergoing some modification, even under the most favourable circumstances, for its preservation. If hops are kept exposed to the air they deteriorate materially; while grain may very well be kept to be employed the next year, hops, on the contrary, will have considerably declined in value, and this chiefly on account of the loss of the volatile oil. The bitter substance which exists in hops does not appear to decrease, the tannic acid gradually diminishes in quantity; and the volatile principle escapes from the plant and spreads in the atmosphere, or partly oxidizes, which gives the hops a disagreeable odour.

Moreover, hops, like the leafy parts of plants, or the parts of the leaves which are not very thick, when they are exposed to contact with the air, are subject to a species of decomposition which on the Continent has received the name of *verwesung*. The plant assumes a dark colour, and all its constituent parts are brought more and more into the dominion of chemical transformation. It has been proposed to dry the hops and then to keep them from contact with the air, which would do away with, or at least lessen, two of the conditions which tend to produce a chemical transformation.

Liebig pronounced in favour of sulphuring hops, and he rightly maintained the innocuity of this simple means of preserving a portion of the plant, which, without it, would rapidly enter into decomposition, and which by these means may be transported and preserved, without declining in value or acquiring any injurious property. He cited in support of his opinion the proposition of Braconnot, to preserve, by means of sulphurous acid, the vegetables employed for domestic use, such as chicory, asparagus, sorrel, &c.

Sulphuring.—To preserve the hops they are usually sulphured, that is, subjected to the action of vapours of burning sulphur, 1 lb. to 2 lbs. of sulphur being employed to 1 cwt. of hops. Old hops are sometimes treated in this manner to impart the colour and appearance of freshly dried hops; but the fraud can be detected by the odour. The best method of testing for sulphur in hops is as follows : A sample of the hops is placed in a sulphuretted hydrogen apparatus, with some zinc and hydrochloric acid; the disengaged gas is passed through a solution of acetate of lead.

If the hops contain sulphurous acid, sulphuretted hydrogen will be disengaged:

$$(SO_2 + 2H_2 + 2H_2O),$$

and black sulphide of lead thrown down from the lead solution. Better still is to receive the disengaged gas in a solution of nitroprusside of sodium, to which a few drops of potash ley have been added; the slightest trace of sulphuretted hydrogen imparts a beautiful purple red colour to the solution. (Wagner.)

Insect Depredators.—Although incidental mention has been made in previous pages of the insect scourges of the hop grower, they may here be briefly summarized. Among the insects injurious to the hop are the caterpillars of the ghost moth (*Hepialus humuli*), which gnaw the roots of the hop plant till the shoots are weakened, and the leaves droop in bright sunshine, the aphides, or plant lice, known as the green fly (*Aphis humuli*), the plant mite, or red spider (*Acarius telarius*), and the wireworm. Curtis says the smaller wireworms are very often the larvæ of *Elater lineatus* and *E. obscurus*, and the larger ones of *E. ruficandis*. Hops in Kent, Worcester, and Herefordshire are often reported to be injured by the wireworm. The Rev. E. Sidney, in a lecture on Parasitic Fungi, published in the 'Journal of the Royal Agricultural Society,' vol. x., p. 394, states that hops are occasionally damaged by an *erysiphe*, having the habits of that of the pea, which seems to be in its early stage a peculiar mould.

The vapour of heated sulphur is usually tried for the red spider, and tobacco water is obnoxious to the aphides.

The scarcity or abundance of the hop crop entirely depends upon the ordinary prevalence or unusual plenty of these pernicious insects. Vain would be the attempt to clear a hop plantation of them, or to rescue any extensive crop from their baneful ravages. Even violent rain has but a partial effect in destroying them.

Production in England.—The growth of hops in Great Britain is almost entirely confined to England, and there chiefly to special localities. The cultivation of this valuable plant does not vary very considerably now from year to year, although affected to some extent by fluctuations of price. Nearly 70,000 acres were returned as planted with hops in England in 1875, the largest acreage ever reached. Hop planting rather declines than otherwise, however, in counties where it is practised upon only a small scale; but the following shows the present acreage and that of seven years previous in the principal districts where it is carried on:

	1868.	1875.
	acres.	acres.
Hants	2,517	3,059
Hereford	5,564	5,984
Kent	41,087	43,614
Surrey	2,208	2,313
Sussex	10,107	11,360
Worcester	2,430	2,468
Other Districts	512	373
Total for England	64,455	69,171
Wales	33	..
	64,488	69,171

About two-thirds of the acreage under hops, it will be seen, is in the county of Kent. The other counties in which hops are planted to any extent are Sussex, Hereford, Worcester, Hants, and Surrey.

The number of acres devoted to the cultivation of hops has long been steadily on the increase since 1693, when they were first successfully cultivated in Kent. The Rev. J. Wilkinson, in the 'Journal of the Royal Agricultural Society,' states, but I know not on what authority, that hops were grown in Kent as early as 1464, but did not come into popular use for more than a century. Indeed the acceptability of our bitter beer is a modern and acquired taste. The Royal Brewer of Eltham was enjoined (temp. Henry VII.) to put neither brimstone nor hops into the ale.

It is perhaps worth the consideration of farmers in some counties where hop planting has not hitherto been introduced, whether it ought not to be tried. The opinion of a geologist, Mr. W. Topley, has been published to the effect that "everywhere below the chalk escarpment hops might probably be cultivated with great success, and the Vale of Pewsey, for instance, would seem especially suited for them."

In 1807 it was found that the hop grounds throughout England amounted to 38,218 acres; this gradually increased till 1819, when it reached 51,000 acres; there was then a slight annual retrogression till 1826, when it reached again 50,471 acres; then ensued a check until 1834, when the tide turned once more; and in 1837 the maximum of the period was reached of 56,323 acres. The same gradual progression and retrogression is noticeable in subsequent years, but in the last nine or ten years the increase has been steady.

The following table gives the acreage under hops officially returned, and the produce per acre, as far as can be ascertained. I have not been able to obtain the acreage for the four years between 1862 and 1866.

Year.	Acres.	Average Growth per Acre.			Year.	Acres.	Average Growth per Acre.		
		cwts.	qrs.	lbs.			cwts.	qrs.	lbs.
1807	38,218	5	1	19	1842	43,752	8	0	4
1808	38,436	13	2	2	1843	43,157	6	1	16
1809	38,357	3	1	17	1844	44,485	6	2	3
1810	38,265	3	3	25	1845	48,057	6	3	6
1811	38,401	8	1	24	1846	51,948	9	2	20
1812	38,700	1	2	15	1847	52,325	8	2	6
1813	39,521	6	3	15	1848	49,232	8	3	20
1814	40,575	7	0	17	1849	42,798	3	3	12
1815	42,150	6	0	9	1850	43,125	11	0	18
1816	44,219	2	0	19	1851	43,244	6	0	22
1817	46,293	2	3	25	1852	46,229	10	3	26
1818	48,593	8	1	27	1853	49,368	6	2	14
1819	51,014	9	3	8	1854	53,823	1	2	15
1820	50,148	5	2	25	1855	57,757	12	3	8
1821	45,662	7	0	1	1856	54,527	9	0	16
1822	43,557	9	2	15	1857	50,974	8	1	14
1823	41,458	1	1	5	1858	47,601	10	0	0
1824	43,449	7	0	11	1859	45,665	15	0	0
1825	46,718	1	0	8	1860	46,272	2	0	17
1826	50,471	11	0	5	1861	47,942	5	0	0
1827	49,485	5	3	14	1862				
1828	48,365	7	1	12	1863				
1829	46,135	1	2	25	1864				
1830	46,726	3	3	17	1865				
1831	47,129	7	2	20	1866				
1832	47,101	6	0	12	1867	64,284			
1833	49,187	6	2	11	1868	64,455			
1834	51,273	7	2	18	1869	61,785			
1835	53,816	9	0	5	1870	60,594			
1836	55,482	7	1	26	1871	60,830			
1837	56,323	6	2	7	1872	61,926			
1838	55,045	6	1	22	1873	63,276			
1839	53,305	8	0	15	1874	65,799			
1840	44,805	1	2	8	1875	69,171			
1841	45,768	6	2	12					

Mr. Lance, in his 'Hop Farmer,' makes some slight difference in the average yields up to 1836, but I prefer quoting the above figures, which up to 1853 are upon the authority of Mr. Baxter, of the 'Sussex Express.' The years from 1854 are computed from the official acreage and duty paid. Since the abolition of the duty only conjectural estimates can be made.

The average produce of hops per acre in England in periods of seven years was therefore as follows:

	Cwts.		Cwts.
1807–1813	5·58	1835–1841	6·29
1814–1820	5·48	1842–1848	7·75
1821–1827	5·62	1849–1855	7·60
1828–1834	5·31	1855–1861	9·75

A hop acre differs from a statute acre, and is considered to comprise a portion of land containing 1000 hop plants placed in rows, 6 or 7 feet apart, and equal, upon an average, to about two-thirds of the statute acre.

The yearly average quantity grown in the ten years ending 1854 was not quite thirty-six millions of pounds, while in the next five years the average annual produce amounted to sixty-one millions of pounds, although upwards of 12,000 acres of ground had been taken out of cultivation for hops since 1855. In the year 1855 there was an aggregate of 57,757 acres of hop land, and a sum of 398,365*l.* was paid as old duty on the hops gathered and cured that season; but in the next four years a considerable extent of hop gardens was grubbed up, and in 1859 duty on 43,729 acres, amounting to 328,070*l.*, was paid to the Inland Revenue, and hop grounds were diminished 14,028 acres. On the total abolition of the duty (an impost which for many years had been a great source of grievance to the hop growers), the gardens were again increased, and have now attained the largest extent ever reached. In Kent, the most extensive hop county in England, hops from 33,000 acres were gathered and cured in 1870, and the early grounds averaged a yield of 14 cwt. to 16 cwt. an acre. Sussex, another important hop-growing district, cultivated 14,500 acres, and produced a yield from

18 cwt. to 22 cwt. an acre; but the crops were materially damaged by the gales in September, and many growths were imperfectly cured. In Berks and Hants, comprising hop districts of an extent of 3300 acres, a yield of 14 cwt. to 18 cwt. was gathered. The Rev. J. Wilkinson, writing on the Farming of Hampshire, states that the average expenses of all kinds for seven years growing hops amounted to 30*l.* per acre per annum. The produce was 12 cwt. per acre. The sorts grown were Grapes, Green bine, and Farnham white bine. Herefordshire had under culture 6000 and Worcestershire 3800 acres, and produced early crops of hops of good qualities, and 15 cwt. to 18 cwt. an acre was gathered. Surrey is productive of a choice quality of hops, celebrated for their bright colour and superior aroma, and other properties essential for brewing pale and bitter beer. Farnham is the chief district. 1100 acres were cultivated in 1870, and from 14 cwt. to 16 cwt. an acre was the average gathered and cured. The other counties contributed 3900 acres of hops.

The free importation of foreign hops to this country and the large continental growths have occasionally decreased the value of home-grown hops. At Weyhill great hop-fair in 1867 the top price obtained for hops was 12*l.* per cwt.; and at the fair in 1870, 7*l.* per cwt. was the highest value made. Many crops were deteriorated in value by the unfavourable picking season, and were imperfectly cured, and diminished in weight; but it was estimated that the crops of the year 1870 were equivalent to the old duty of 450,000*l.*

The 'Brewers' Journal,' in pronouncing an opinion upon

the hop crop of 1872, estimated "the out-turn at about 350,000*l.* old duty, and this would give an average of from 10½ to 11 cwt. per acre all round. Kent and Sussex, with Surrey and Hampshire, had some 56,000 acres between them, perhaps more, and we must not forget that the Government returns are neither complete nor reliable.* We place the acreage at 65,000 for all England, and some experienced Kent farmers agree with our estimate—nay, we have heard it set as high as 70,000; but this is clearly too much. Now, we must remember when weighing the crop upon the poles that there are 1200 hills to the acre, each hill having three poles. Well, let us consider that we have these heavily-laden poles, some in Kent and Sussex 14 feet high, some in Farnham 16 feet and 18 feet out of the ground, and it may be stated that one bushel to the hill (not pole) is not an extravagant assessment. Then we come to the following figures: 80 bushels to the cwt. gives 15 cwt. per acre, 90 bushels about 13 cwt. per acre, and 100 bushels 12 cwt. per acre. There are some large tracts where this must have been exceeded, and, having studied this always difficult problem with a calm and unbiassed mind, we consider that we are dealing very reasonably when we place our idea of the old duty at the 350,000*l.* quoted above."

Opinions vary as to the extent of the yield of 1875. In some places the hops which were much spoiled by mould came down light; while in others they were perfection itself,

* Papers on the hop district of Farnham, by Mr. H. Evershed, may be consulted in the 'Journal of the Royal Agricultural Society of England,' vol. xiv., p. 406; and on the acreage yield of hops in Hampshire, by the Rev. J. Wilkinson, *ibid.*, vol. xxii., p. 303.

being full of flower, bright, and clean, so that a crop of from 15 cwt. to 20 cwt. per acre was not an uncommon estimate for the season. Allowing for small, or no crops at all, in certain blighted districts, Messrs. Bakers, White, and Morgan, in their circular, estimated the English growth to be equal to 420,000*l.* old duty, or more than thrice the amount yielded in 1874.

In order to give the current opinion of other experienced parties, I quote the following different statements.

Mr. M. Bruce Tate, manager of the Hop Exchange, London, writes:

" The season commences with relatively high prices, which may be ascribed to the following causes: (1) The absence of good quality, and the reduced stocks generally of old hops; (2) our new crop being much below an average; (3) an undoubtedly small crop in Germany, and short crops on the Continent generally.

" As the result of a careful investigation, I should estimate our home growth to yield some 350,000 to 380,000 cwt., and the continental crop, all through, at about one-third of a full average. America is reported to have equal to about two-thirds of last year's growth, the quality being various, or 'uneven.'

" It will be a natural deduction from the foregoing that foreign supplies to this country must be unusually small; in fact, I rather anticipate the probability of hops being exported to the Continent. Under any circumstances, price at this moment is alone a bar to business in German hops on this side. That America and Belgium will have hops enough and to spare, there is little doubt; still, German dealers have already been making, and will doubtless continue to make, free purchases from both countries, thereby diverting from this kingdom supplies which otherwise would have come here.

"As regards quality, the English crop is far in advance of last year. We shall have a fair sprinkling of fine, coloury stuff, with a full proportion of good medium, whilst really low quality will be comparatively absent, unless mould, which is more or less present in many districts, spreads to any serious extent; but as picking is now rapidly progressing, the chances are against its doing so.

"Weighing carefully the general estimate of probabilities in connection with this market, I am not induced to fear any retrograde movement in prices, but rather to place faith in an upward tendency.

"As values have hardly settled down yet, the following quotations must be regarded as more or less nominal, more especially in regard to foreign :

Kent, Mid and East	8*l.* to	12*l.*
Weald of Kent..	7*l.* „	9*l.* 9*s.*
Sussex	6*l.* „	7*l.* 10*s.*
Farnham..	9*l.* „	11*l.*
German—Market hops	14*l.* „	20*l.*
Belgian—Poperinghe	7*l.* „	7*l.* 5*s.*
Alost	6*l.* 10*s.* „	7*l.*"

A hop grower, in the 'Mark Lane Express,' writing under date September 26, 1876, observes:

"Picking being now over, something like an accurate estimate of the crop can be formed. This is arrived at from statistics of each parish in every hop-growing district, the probable result being as follows, viz.:

District.	Acres.	Yield per Acre.	Total.
		cwts.	cwts.
Mid Kent	17,000	7	119,000
East Kent	12,000	$6\frac{1}{2}$	78,000
West and North Kent	4,000	3	12,000
Weald of Kent	10,000	6	60,000
Sussex	11,000	5	55,000
Worcester and Hereford	9,000	$1\frac{1}{2}$	13,500
Surrey and Hants	5,500	6	33,000
Total	68,500	..	370,500

Or equal to an old duty of 185,500*l*.

" Now, as to the foreign crops, I hold a circular under date 14th September, issued by a leading brewers' house, in which it states: 'Of the continental crops very little need be said; they are short everywhere, and in some parts—in Bohemia, for instance—there is almost an entire failure. A good general continental crop would probably yield, say about 1,000,000 to 1,200,000 cwt.; the aggregate estimate of this year's produce is 260,000 to 300,000 cwt.; the estimated annual consumption is set down at about from 550,000 to 600,000 cwt.; the stock on hand, including that with brewers, is assumed to be between 150,000 and 180,000 cwt. It is therefore not improbable that foreign merchants will be buyers on our market, rather than sellers; and we may here note that already a considerable demand is reported at New York for Bavaria, where prices of their growth are far above ours.'

" Having dealt with the home and foreign crops, let us

turn our attention to the stocks of old hops on hand. It is said that brewers hold largely of yearlings: probably they do; but if so, no one else does. Growers never held fewer, and the London merchants are admittedly bare of good coloured hops, the chief supply being low in colour, but, at same time, good, useful porter-brewing sorts, which will be wanted by-and-bye for consumptive purposes. If we look beyond yearlings for a supply it must be disappointing, there being little or nothing left. The coming consumption, therefore, will necessarily be upon the new crop and yearlings; and putting them together, what is it to meet a large and growing demand for home and foreign requirements? Another point must not be lost sight of, viz. the crop of excellent barley, which is already selling at very favourable prices for the brewers."

A writer in the 'Chambers of Agriculture Journal,' in September, thus speaks of the home and foreign hop plantations in 1876:

"Another hop season has passed away, which has been marked in its course by somewhat unusual vicissitudes. It has differed totally from that of 1875, which will be remembered as having produced an enormous crop of indifferent quality; but it may be said to be more like that of 1868, which was also a year of heat and drought. In that year, however, persistent attacks of red spider caused a short crop. In this year aphis blight has reduced the amount grown to less than half that of the abundant yield of last year. The bine came away weakly and backward in the spring, as the plants were, no doubt, somewhat exhausted by the heavy crop of the previous season. The Grapes, which are usually much more strong and hardy than the Goldings, were especially sleek of bine, 'spindly,' and sickly-looking in all districts; in many places these were not tied, as they would not furnish, until June, and in some cases not even then. Then came the aphides in swarms, which further affected the delicate plants and kept them back, so that a portion of the bine hardly reached the summit of the poles. In parts of the plantation the aphides remained steadily, and multiplied excessively, so that a regular black blight ensued, which ruined the chances of a good crop in Herefordshire, Worcestershire, North Kent, West Kent, the Weald of Kent, and Sussex, with a portion of the Hampshire country. Though Mid Kent, East Kent, and Farnham were visited by the plague of flies, which duly bred lice, these disappeared as if by magic, just as the planters were getting their washing engines in order, and inquiring the price of soft soap, and it was curious to see part of the plantations in Kent black and blasted by blight, while the other part was green, and comparatively luxuriant. All districts, however, were deficient in bine; even in East Kent, which has held the sway easily throughout the whole season, the bine was not over plentiful at any time, while the Grape bine in all the Mid Kent district was 'platty' and short throughout, so that it was impossible that a large crop could have been grown had the weather been different. The heat and drought hindered the growth of the weak bine in a degree, and prevented the action of the artificial manures, such as rape dust, guano, and patent hop manures, that were plentifully applied to force it up the poles. At one time these extreme weather influences were affecting all the hop plants, even those upon the Kentish rag, which generally stand any amount of heat; and if the welcome showers had not come in the last week of August, the crop must have been very far short of that which has been realized. Notwithstanding the dryness of the atmosphere for eight or nine weeks together, mould was very troublesome, and threatened to run fast when the hop cones were developed. Enormous quantities of sulphur were applied, in many instances four or five applications of it were made, which seemed to be of no avail until the wet came, when the mould, as a rule, was stayed, except in parts of East Kent, and here and there in Mid Kent. Mould literally defied sulphur in a few spots in East Kent, where some acres were left unpicked in consequence of its ravages. Generally speaking, the cultivation of the hop plantations was not so good as usual in the winter and early spring, nor was the manuring so liberal, for the planters as a body had lost much money by the last two crops, and this may in some degree account for the bad start made by the bine.

"The winter of 1875–6 was very wet, and not at all suited to the cultivation of heavy land; the early spring was also wet, and the long spell of dry weather came upon the planters before they had succeeded in properly working the rain-battered soil, and in obtaining a good tiller for the rootlets and fibres. Clay lands in the Weald of Kent and Sussex were very rough and cloddy throughout the whole summer, and there was no chance of penetrating the surface or of pulverizing the clods before the fibres were fairly dried up. Planters assiduously washed the plants in many cases in the worst blighted districts. Some washed as many as four or five times, and were rewarded for their perseverance with a crop of from 4 to 5 cwt. per acre. Others took the chances of the blight going away in time to allow the plants to recover; but in most cases recovery came too late, and the bine had been too completely exhausted by its enemies to make a fresh start when the showers arrived.

"Though the rains came late, they were of infinite service to the healthier part of the plantation, and added considerably to the amount of its produce; for even on the best soils, upon the ragstone, of which it is said that the hop plants there would not suffer in a summer quite without rain, there were evident signs of flagging energies. Rain, however plentiful and grateful, cannot make bine at the end of August; all it did was to make the late bur grow out into goodly hops, and to cause the hops that were developed to become larger and better conditioned. There were great complaints of blind bine, and of the tendency of the bur to dry up and fall off, particularly in the Goldings, and the rains came just soon enough to stop this generally. In Sussex the rain increased the crop most materially, by causing every blossom, every tiny bur, to turn into a fine sized hop. Blight had vanished in East Sussex before the rain, and the plants were in a fit state to derive all the advantages it could give.

"A much better crop has been grown in the whole of the Eastern Division of the county than any thought possible in the early part of August. Tons an acre have been grown in a few lucky spots, and the average of this district was about 7 cwt. per acre. The whole average for this county was much reduced by the small quantity grown in the

Western Division, where blight steadily held its ground throughout the season.

"Very good returns for the year were made at Rye, Peasmarsh, Northam, Brightling, Ticehurst, Wadhurst, Lamberhurst, and other parishes where the farming is generally high. The East Kent plantations suffered but little from blight. Mould vexed them considerably, so that pieces of hops were left unpicked here and there; but, taking it round, this district grew more per acre than any other, and with some few exceptions its produce is of fair quality and of brilliant colour. About 8 cwt. per acre, it is thought, has been grown here. Some parishes where the cultivation was very good, as it always is, yielded from 9 cwt. to 12 cwt. per acre. Among these Bobbing, Faversham, Rainham, Hackington, Hardres, Petham, Selling, Chilham, may be cited, while the Ashford and the bastard East Kent districts were not so productive. In point of quality West Kent ranks next, having yielded an average crop of 7 cwt. per acre, of very good quality. The neighbourhood of Maidstone was much favoured. Excellent lots of Goldings of superior merit were obtained at West and East Farleigh, Linton, Otham, Langley, Zalding, Wateringbury, Mereworth, Hunton; some good managers in these villages having grown as much as 10 cwt. round. North and West Kent were hard hit by blight, and have hardly produced 4 cwt. per acre. About 6 cwt. per acre were grown in the usually prolific Weald of Kent, where blight did infinite mischief. Near Farnham town the hop gardens escaped blight, mould, and all disorder. Bine was not over plentiful, but about 8 cwt. of choice hops were gathered there. The rest of the Surrey and Hants gardens were more or less blighted, and the whole return of the 5500 acres has been estimated at about 6 cwt. per acre. No more than from 1 to 1¼ cwt. per acre can be claimed for the Worcestershire and Herefordshire plantations, for the aphides grievously tormented them from May till August, so that they never had the ghost of a chance to get away.

"Putting the acreage of the United Kingdom at 68,500 acres, which is very near the mark, the following table, giving the acreage of each district and its yield, will show the total amount of hops grown this year (1876):

District.	Acreage.	Yield per Acre.	Total Amount.
		cwts.	cwts.
East Kent	12,000	8	96,000
Mid Kent	17,000	7	119,000
North Kent	1,000	5	5,000
West Kent	3,000	4	12,000
Weald of Kent	10,000	6	60,000
Sussex	11,000	6	66,000
Worcester and Hereford	9,000	1	9,000
Surrey and Hants	5,500	6	33,000
Total	68,500	..	400,000

Equal to an old duty of 200,000*l*., or an average of close upon 6 cwt. for each acre in cultivation; rather less than the amount of an average crop. Partisans of the planters hold that considerably less than this has been realized; partisans of the consumers, or of the merchants, hold that it is far under the mark.

"The 'Times' correspondent, writing on hops, puts the yield at some 600,000 cwt. this year; an estimate absurd and ridiculous, as unfortunately is too often the case, in the eyes of all who know how short the hops came down everywhere, and how very many bushels were required for a pocket, not only at the commencement but throughout the picking season.

"Considering all the drawbacks of the year, drought, mould, and exhaustion, it must be said that the return of 6 cwt. per acre all round is wonderful, and it is certain that it has not been exceeded by a pound.

"Throughout the whole of the Continent the hop crop has been short. With the exception of Belgium, no continental district has produced anything like an average return. In Bavaria, Wurtemberg, Baden, Alsace, Galicia, Lorraine, and Burgundy, not half of an average quantity was grown; and in Bohemia, in the celebrated provinces of Saatz, Auscha, and Dauba, nothing like this quantity was obtained.

"Black blight, red spider, and drought made sad havoc in Austria, Germany, and France; the bine came away weak and unkindly, and could not grow away from its numerous foes. Prices are very high at all the German and French markets, and higher still in those of Austria. From 13*l.* 10*s.* to 16*l.* 15*s.* are the prices now current at Nuremberg, and from 17*l.* to 25*l.* at Saatz.

"German merchants are already in the English and American markets, endeavouring to make good the deficiencies of their home supply.

"The Belgian growth is the same as that of the English, about 6 cwt. per acre. There was a general attack of aphis blight in the early summer, but it cleared away in time to allow the plant to recover, and grew a moderate quantity. Prices run from 6*l.* to 8*l.* for Belgian hops.

"The latest accounts from America state that previous estimates of 140,000 bales as the amount of the year's yield in that country will not be realized, and that the quality is not so good as last year's. Planters find that the hops have not come down according to their expectation in many of the States. Prices at present are about 1s. 3d. to 1s. 4d. per lb. There will be a considerable surplus for exportation to England and Germany, but nothing like the quantity, 50,000 bales, that were exported last year to England from New York."

QUANTITY OF HOPS CHARGED AND AMOUNT OF DUTY PAID IN ENGLAND for each Year from the Imposition of the Duty to its Repeal.

The Number of Acres under Cultivation will be found on page 62.

Years.	No. of Pounds.	Amount of Duty.	Years.	No. of Pounds.	Amount of Duty.
	Commenced June 1, 1711.				£ s. d.
		£ s. d.	1735	10,316,090	42,989 17 2
1711	12,064,578	50,323 19 5	1736	11,133,618	46,396 8 11
1712	7,262,890	30,282 8 8	1737	13,618,943	56,751 2 0
1713	5,530,571	23,057 1 8	1738	20,961,698	87,349 14 8
1714	3,466,419	14,463 19 9	1739	16,976,625	70,742 18 8
1715	10,792,163	44,981 6 5	1740	9,091,226	37,889 15 7
1716	4,882,067	20,355 5 9	1741	17,983,569	74,945 6 11
1717	13,108,749	54,644 13 2	1742	10,916,218	45,484 10 7
1718	3,600,890	15,005 16 3	1743	15,329,731	63,899 7 3
1719	21,664,980	90,319 13 7	1744	11,210,849	46,713 1 5
1720	9,158,795	38,174 12 9	1745	8,338,614	34,750 19 10
1721	14,763,819	61,536 18 9	1746	22,063,454	91,952 0 1
1722	11,937,956	49,759 6 6	1747	15,159,786	63,184 10 6
1723	7,266,041	30,282 9 6	1748	20,950,964	87,315 9 2
1724	14,687,559	61,221 0 0	1749	8,713,436	36,326 8 9
1725	1,565,891	6,531 12 0	1750	17,323,123	72,186 6 3
1726	20,391,638	85,018 10 5	1751	17,796,648	74,158 4 0
1727	16,659,259	69,422 12 11	1752	19,724,648	82,190 16 10
1728	9,954,830	41,496 9 10	1753	21,875,072	91,180 4 10
1729	11,625,922	48,463 0 10	1754	26,962,204	112,353 13 10
1730	10,636,152	44,345 9 5	1755	19,819,830	82,587 18 6
1731	5,583,380	23,278 14 2	1756	11,522,851	48,027 0 10
1732	8,407,933	35,045 13 4	1757	16,749,242	69,807 16 1
1733	16,868,256	70,311 12 8	1758	17,505,552	72,998 0 7
1734	8,986,943	37,448 19 7			

CULTURE AND PRODUCTION IN ENGLAND. 77

QUANTITY OF HOPS CHARGED AND AMOUNT OF DUTY PAID, &c.—*continued.*

Years.	No. of Pounds.	Amount of Duty. £ s. d.	Years.	No. of Pounds.	Amount of Duty. £ s. d.
1759	10,107,026	42,113 19 11	1804	37,069,609	386,316 16 7
1760	28,437,135	118,521 16 11	1805	6,860,557	57,223 14 8
1761	19,607,489	81,781 7 4	1806	31,959,046	266,452 3 9
1762	18,992,809	79,145 6 6	1807	20,899,826	174,210 13 1
1763	21,203,565	88,356 12 6	1808	52,588,276	438,316 2 2
1764	4,138,688	17,261 6 7	1809	13,359,171	111,337 4 6
1765	17,751,602	73,969 16 6	1810	15,341,747	127,879 1 1
1766	27,987,764	116,627 8 3	1811	32,784,852	273,242 14 8
1767	6,244,727	26,043 3 9	1812	6,406,695	53,352 7 5
1768	27,440,225	114,364 14 5	1813	27,441,818	228,739 14 1
1769	3,890,627	16,212 3 3	1814	29,328,458	244,430 13 0
1770	24,299,157	101,248 5 10	1815	25,862,540	215,569 16 8
1771	7,967,810	33,217 19 7	1816	9,663,842	80,637 6 3
1772	24,617,747	102,584 10 2	1817	13,882,904	115,720 0 10
1773	11,013,453	45,901 15 5	1818	41,628,396	346,959 14 3
1774	33,320,210	138,854 6 2	1819	50,510,920	421,146 17 4
1775	10,004,388	41,708 1 10	1820	28,911,841	240,940 11 11
1776	30,196,172	125,825 4 7	1821	31,781,986	264,859 9 7
1777	10,500,694	43,761 17 3	1822	42,549,915	354,587 15 4
1778	38,416,457	160,101 10 3	1823	5,434,145	45,689 15 11
1779	12,737,916	53,086 4 8	1824	31,162,255	259,685 9 2
1780	27,927,770	116,338 3 3	1825	5,078,596	42,444 15 4
1781	25,861,344	107,770 6 5	1826	57,227,487	477,375 13 5
1782	3,112,308	12,968 12 5	1827	29,425,342	245,353 11 4
1783	15,801,792	65,861 2 2	1828	35,887,242	299,060 7 0
1784	19,736,202	82,238 6 11	1829	8,013,808	66,781 14 9
1785	23,519,267	98,019 1 6	1830	18,462,003	153,850 0 7
1786	19,996,055	83,330 2 1	1831	36,500,028	304,166 18 0
1787	8,813,819	42,259 5 5	1832	29,012,406	241,770 1 0
1788	29,978,410	143,732 18 2	1833	32,747,311	272,894 5 2
1789	21,176,855	101,480 11 4	1834	39,587,497	329,895 16 2
1790	22,308,245	106,908 11 10	1835	49,086,709	409,055 18 3
1791	18,867,548	90,410 7 1	1836	41,874,913	348,957 12 2
1792	33,949,732	162,682 11 7	1837	37,295,304	310,794 4 0
1793	5,000,175	23,971 12 8	1838	35,801,224	298,343 10 10
1794	42,528,587	203,790 6 2	1839	42,898,629	357,488 11 6
1795	17,180,497	82,346 14 7	1840	7,114,917	362,255 10 5
1796	15,739,511	75,476 7 9	1841	30,504,108	266,908 6 0
1797	32,881,264	157,655 18 2	1842	35,432,143	310,029 0 3
1798	11,774,587	56,425 1 3	1843	27,862,730	243,796 8 1
1799	15,293,335	73,286 16 6	1844	29,285,094	256,243 0 5
1800	15,229,379	73,228 12 9	1845	32,974,750	288,526 10 5
1801	50,402,257	241,867 4 0	1846	50,704,030	443,657 9 6
1802	3,223,869	33,624 4 0	1847	45,134,367	394,921 14 0
1803	41,264,001	430,032 0 11	1848	44,343,985	388,007 17 5

QUANTITY OF HOPS CHARGED AND AMOUNT OF DUTY PAID, &c.—*continued*.

Years.	No. of Pounds.	Amount of Duty. £ s. d.	Years.	No. of Pounds.	Amount of Duty. £ s. d.
1849	16,650,915	145,693 4 9	1856	55,868,927	488,850 9 3
1850	48,537,668	424,702 3 0	1857	47,717,561	417,526 2 4
1851	27,042,919	236,623 1 10	1858	53,125,100	464,842 3 10
1852	51,102,494	447,143 9 11	1859	68,496,958	599,346 2 7
1853	31,751,693	277,807 9 10	1860	11,162,777	69,767 7 1
1854	9,877,126	86,422 14 1	1861	23,952,087	149,700 10 10
1855	83,221,304	728,183 14 3			Repealed June 3, 1862.

The rate of duty from 1711 to 1777 was 1d. per lb.
   ,,   ,,   1778 ,, 1779 ,, 1d. ,, and 5 per cent.
   ,,   ,,   1780 ,, 1782 ,, 1d. ,, ,, 10 ,,
   ,,   ,,   1783 ,, 1785 ,, 1d. ,, ,, 15 ,,
   ,,   ,,   1786 ,, 1801 ,, 1d. $\frac{12}{20}$ of a farthing per lb.
   ,,   ,,   1802 ,, 1804 ,, 2½d. per lb.
   ,,   ,,   1805 ,, 1839 ,, 2d. ,,
   ,,   ,,   1840 ,, 1859 ,, 2d. ,, and 5 per cent. additional.
   ,,   ,,   1860 ,, 1861 ,, 1½d. ,,

No duty was charged on hops in Scotland, and the duty did not extend to Ireland.

By a calculation, made from reliable sources, of the outlay paid for labour in picking, drying, and preparing the hops for market, it will be seen how large a sum of money is put into circulation for labour, &c., in the process of hop gathering. Assuming the number of pockets grown at 530,000, there would be paid in round figures—

	£
Picking (105 bushels to each pocket), at 6 bushels for 1s.	463,234
Binman, each pocket 2s.	52,941
Measurer, poke boy, and bookkeeper, at 1s. ..	26,470
Wear and tear of pokes and bin cloths, &c., at 6d.	13,235
Drying and treading, at 2s. 6d.	66,177
Sulphur, at 6d.	13,235
Fuel, at 1s. 3d.	
Cloth for packing, at 3s.	79,412
Carting and drawing, at 2s. 3d.	59,559
Insurance, at 3d.	6,617
Total	£780,880

Hop Pickers.—To give some idea of the number of people employed in picking hops, the following is an official return, kindly furnished me by the Secretary of the South-Eastern Railway, for the last twelve years, of the number of hop pickers conveyed both up and down by special trains from and to London; no account being taken of those who travelled by ordinary trains:

	From London.	Returned.
1865	11,090	12,000
1866	11,000	13,000
1867	8,777	10,694
1868	14,476	17,288
1869	12,522	13,458
1870	15,945	16,915
1871	8,221	10,839
1872	15,947	17,233
1873	14,664	16,933
1874	8,929	10,933
1875	16,010	16,412
1876	14,008	16,352

A writer in 'Land and Water' thus speaks of hop picking:

"There is something wonderfully soothing in the aroma of the hop. The pickers sleep well in the little huts or tents they have run up; and the babies we have seen swinging in their hammocks between the tall bines under an open network of strobiles are invariably in the arms of Morpheus. The hop is classed as a narcotic, and there are many kinds grown—the 'red bine,' 'green bine,' and 'white bine.' The first produces small cones, but is said to resist the attack of insects best of any; the green bine will stand poor ground, and the white bine is the most difficult to grow. It is also the one that realizes the highest market price. The hops emit a very powerful scent when ripe for picking, and all good experienced growers watch for this peculiar odour, and begin at once. They pay more attention to this point than to the appearance of the hops. The wild hop is a very pretty, graceful climbing plant, but not equal to the cultivated female plant. It looks well in our hedges mixed with some of the beautiful autumnal berries that ripen about October; but I am not aware that it is ever used medicinally. King Pepin is said to have been the first person (of whom there is any record) to have mentioned hops, and the passage occurs in a letter of donation, in which his Majesty speaks of 'humuloraiæ'; but I fancy he will be better remembered in France for his efforts to conciliate Pope Gregory and the organ he presented to the Church of St. Corneille at Compiegne, than as the proprietor of a hop garden."

CULTIVATION AND PRODUCTION IN EUROPE. 81

CHAPTER VI.

CULTIVATION AND PRODUCTION ON THE CONTINENT OF
EUROPE.

As the consumption of beer in most countries increases daily, so the production of hops necessarily makes equal progress.

At the recent Exhibition of Scientific Apparatus and Educational Appliances, held at South Kensington in 1876, there was shown a most interesting general map of the hop-growing districts of Central Europe, by J. Carl and C. Homan, of Nuremberg. There were also shown special maps of several of the principal continental hop-growing countries; an "agrarian, statistical, and general map of the European hop-growing districts on the Continent and in England;" "tabular geographical representations of the cultivation of hops and of the hop consumption of the whole world," with a classification of the various sorts of hops, and comparative tables of the agrarian measures and commercial weights. These maps were exceedingly interesting, as showing the locality and extent of cultivation of a plant so important as the hop.

According to the statistics exhibited at the Scientific Col-

G

lection and at South Kensington in 1876, there were under hops in Europe as follows:

	Hectares (of 2½ acres).	Production.
		cwts.
Germany	37,910	477,111
Austria	7,711	92,532
Belgium	6,500	97,500
France	4,000	48,000
Rest of Europe	619	8,454
England	25,696	384,090
	82,436	1,107,687

The following, however, appears to me to be the true acreage under hops in various countries, as far as can be ascertained with any degree of precision, at the latest period:

	Year.	Acres.
Great Britain	1875	69,171
Bavaria	1873	51,823
Wurtemberg	1874	12,525
Baden	1872	4,200
Belgium	1871	10,000
Holland	1874	474
France	1872	9,223
Austria	1871	17,770
United States		20,000
Tasmania	1871	561
Victoria & New Zealand	1875	126

It is worthy of notice in connection with the extent of the liquor traffic in this country, that the English consumption of hops is by far the greatest of any country, for while England shows a consumption of 600,000 cwt., Germany, the next largest, gives only 321,000 cwt., and Austria 100,000 cwt., the remaining countries decreasing in quantity much more rapidly.

ON THE CONTINENT OF EUROPE.

WURTEMBERG.—The culture of hops in Wurtemberg has occupied a great degree of attention in the last ten years, so that the culture now extends over 12,000 acres, and is on the increase. Owing to the favourable conditions of soil and climate, the use of an excellent system of poles and iron wire, combined with skilful and rational processes of culture, the produce is generally in demand in wholesale commerce, and the export reaches a large figure. At the Paris Exhibition of 1867 there were forty-six exhibitors of hops from Wurtemberg, and at Vienna, in 1873, there was an equally good display.

The following statement shows the extent and produce of hop cultivation in Wurtemberg in the twenty-one years ending with 1873. The hectare is about 2½ English acres :

	Acreage.	Total Produce.	Produce per Hectare.	Quality.
	hectares.	cwts.	cwts.	
1853	820·7	9,778	7·91	3·02
1854	873·0	2,227	2·55	3·60
1855	706·9	10,572	14·96	2·27
1856	820·7	8,255	10·06	2·63
1857	873·0	11,664	13·34	2·75
1858	975·5	7,979	8·18	3·30
1859	1085·5	16,850	15·52	2·72
1860	1304·5	13,138	10·07	3·40
1861	1664·1	15,903	9·56	3·40
1862	1875·3	32,969	17·58	2·65
1863	2200·2	31,307	14·24	3·09
1864	2484·2	30,668	12·35	3·20
1865	2966·4	39,742	13·40	2·60
1866	3800·7	34,623	9·11	3·50
1867	4665·2	78,256	16·78	2·10
1868	5142·7	81,634	15·87	3·00
1869	5030·5	39,773	7·91	3·50
1870	5118·1	70,692	13·81	3·09
1871	4769·9	36,404	7·63	2·50
1872	4813·9	60,702	12·61	3·30
1873	4900·3	73,733	15·04	2·80

The degrees of quality in the foregoing table are indicated by the following figures: 1 is first-rate; 2, very good; 3, good; 4, middling; 5, inferior. The decimals show the approximation to the class below.

Reducing these to English weights and measures we find the statistics to be as follows:

Years.	Acres.	Produce.
		lbs.
1867	11,515	8,704,672
1870	12,666	7,521,584
1872	11,883	6,798,626
1873	12,103	7,845,152
1874	12,525	5,680,416

The total produce of hops in Wurtemberg was in 1873 73,733 cwt., and as about 25,000 cwt. are required for home consumption, the quantity available for exportation was 48,000 cwt.

Wurtemberg hops have a high reputation in neighbouring countries, as is proved by the success of the Wurtemberg hop growers at Huguenau, where out of seventeen exhibitors thirteen received prizes.

The principal hop-growing districts are those of Rottenburg, in the Black Forest, and the Neckarkreis. The harvest of 1875, 5000 hectares laid down, was below the average of twenty years; the quality, however, was good, and though reports of promising crops in England and America caused sales to be made at the beginning of the season at the low price of 6*l*. per cwt., on the failure of the foreign crops prices rose to 14*l*. 10*s*., and remained at 12*l*. 10*s*., which would give a value for the whole crop of a little over 600,000*l*. sterling.

OTHER GERMAN STATES.—Hops in former times were grown in Brandenbourg, Pomerania, Saxony, and Silesia, but of late years the culture has been greatly extended, principally in Neu Tomysl (province of Posen), where hops have been grown since the seventeenth century, but then only in small quantity. Now the annual crop is large, the quality equal to the hops of Bohemia and Bavaria, and the districts which participate in this culture enjoy a degree of independence formerly unknown, for an average crop represents a capital of one million and a half thalers, or nearly a quarter of a million sterling. In the province of Posen the land under culture with hops is upwards of 6000 acres, and continues to progress. The other provinces only grow enough for home consumption, in the manufacture of common beer, Posen alone exporting largely to foreign countries. The quantity of hops annually produced in Posen is estimated at 40,000 or 50,000 cwt.

The improved culture of hops and the commerce in this product, which is now carried on at Neu Tomysl (province of Posen), and its neighbourhood, dates from 1838. At that period there was only grown about 300 cwt. of hops of an inferior quality, now a good crop yields 40,000 cwt. In 1860, when the crop only yielded 20,000 cwt., the receipts were 2,200,000 thalers; in 1867 the crop was 40,000 cwt.

The growth of hops is almost the sole means of existence of a population of about 10,000 souls, and has brought ease and comfort to the country, otherwise poor. The sale is for the most part made to the hop dealers of Bavaria and Bohemia.

The following figures give the imports of hops into Hamburg for a series of years :

	Centners or Cwts.			Centners or Cwts.
1860	 26,738		1867	 79,597
1861	 59,235		1868	 98,280
1862	 52,875		1869	 72,623
1863	 54,119		1870	 45,266
1864	 25,107		1871	 88,528
1865	 26,058		1872	 50,010
1866	 34,821		1873	 71,619

BAVARIA.—The hop plant is cultivated to a considerable extent in Bavaria, particularly in the circles of Rezat and the Upper Danube; the quantity raised varies, but has reached 134,000 cwt. a year, of which about half is exported.

In 1863 there were 43,531 acres under hops, which produced 15,090,992 lbs.; since then the acreage under hops has increased to nearly 52,000 acres

The hops of Spalt are the best, and the German and French brewers who make beer which has to be kept long are obliged to employ Spalt hops with those of Saatz in Austria, which are the finest and most aromatic hops grown. These products are of a high reputation, and are the Chateau Lafitte, the Clos Vougent, and the Johannisberg, as it were, of hops of Continental growths. Bavarian growths most resemble English hops.

The districts where hops are grown in Bavaria are as follows : Spalt (town and rural district), Kindengen and Heidak, Holledau, Hersbruck and neighbourhood, Altdorf, Lauf, Sultzbach, Aisch and Zeimgrund, Bamberg and Forchheim, Franken and Wasserburg; and in Bohemia, Saatz (town and district), Auscha, Dauba grunland, and other districts.

The hop cultivation in Bavaria now occupies 51,823 acres, and the system of wire-fencing instead of hop poles is gradually spreading, though the drying is still done without artificial heat in the sun instead of kilns. Nuremberg is the chief market for hops for all Germany, and from 60 to 70 million marks (½ lb.) of hops are sold there every year.

The following was an estimate of the foreign production of hops made four or five years ago, in cwts.:

BAVARIA.

	Centners.
Spalt, town district	2,100
Spalt, rural district	16,000
Kindengen and Heidak	7,000
Holledau	25,000
Hersbruck and neighbourhood	12,000
Altdorf	9,000
Lauf	6,000
Sultzbach	8,000
Aisch and Zeimgrund	20,000
Bamberg and Forchheim	12,000
Franken and Wasserburg	6,500
Total	133,600

To which had to be added—

	Centners.
Saatz, town	1,500
Saatz, district	20,000
Auscha	25,000
Dauba grunland	30,000
Other districts	8,500
Total for Bohemia	85,000
Upper Austria	9,000
Prussian Poland	18,000
Altmark and Brunswick	20,000
Baden	13,000
Wurtemberg	25,000
Total Germany	303,600
France	40,000
Belgium	80,000
Total Continent	423,600
The United States of America	50,000
Total crop of foreign hops	473,600

Besides Bavaria and Bohemia, the chief European countries producing hops, it will be seen, are Upper Austria, Pomerania, Prussian Poland, Altmark and Brunswick, Baden, Wurtemberg, France, and Belgium.

BADEN.—In the Duchy of Baden the produce of hops is increasing. In 1867, 30,000 cwt. were sold in Mannheim for 1,500,000 florins, against 20,000 cwt. in 1866. Fears are, however, entertained of an unfavourable nature sooner or later, owing to the immense increase in the cultivation of hops in all countries.

There are now 4235 morgen of land under culture with hops. The morgen is equal to 0·8896 acre.

The hop trade of Baden is of great extent and importance, the average crop in good years being about 23,000 cwt. It is carried on in Mannheim by about 25 persons. About half the produce goes to Bavaria, Bohemia, France, England, Spain, and Portugal, and the other half is consumed in the country and in the other states of the Zollverein. The three first-named countries take the best-quality hops, and England the most ordinary sorts. The large hop trade with Bavaria and Bohemia is the result of the improvement in the cultivation of hops in Baden, which has taken place of late years.

AUSTRIA.—In 1870 there were 17,770 acres under hop culture in Austria, which produced 7,710,444 lbs. In 1871 the yield in Upper Austria was 9,403,856 lbs.

A pamphlet recently published by Herr Noback, of Prague, stated that the total number of breweries in the Cisleithan provinces, Austria, which in 1860 were 2794, in 1869 were reduced to 2471; in spite of this falling off in the number of breweries, the annual production of beer had increased from 11,495,723 eimers (18 gallons) to 13,984,132 eimers. Bohemia alone produces 5,650,085 eimers; Lower Austria, 3,435,953 eimers; Moravia, 1,463,310; the provinces on the Adriatic coast, 2692. In Hungary, Transylvania, Croatia, and Slavonia, there were, in 1869, 318 breweries, producing 989,532 eimers; and in the frontier provinces, 31 breweries, producing 51,154 eimers. The total production of beer throughout the whole empire was 15,024,818 eimers, and the number of breweries 2820.

In Hungary wooden pegs or short stakes are driven into the ground at such distances apart as it is intended to plant the vines; and at longer distances—usually about 20 to 25 yards—light poles are erected, with a height of from 12 to 15 feet above the surface, so that there are parallel lines all over the ground of short stakes or pegs placed at certain distances, and projecting about 8 to 12 inches in height, while parallel rows of poles, from 12 to 13 feet high, cross these at right angles, and at from 20 to 25 yards distance apart. A stout wire is stretched horizontally from pole to pole all over the ground, while vertical wires, or tight rope, made of any suitable material, are attached to the pegs and carried up and fastened to the horizontal wires, thus offering a steady support to the hop vines during the period of growth. At harvest time the ropes are detached and carried to the picking stage with the vines, and the field cleared for the usual tillage operations, without the trouble and expense of shifting, stacking, and resetting the poles.

This plan has been introduced into Wurtemberg, Baden, Bavaria, and other hop-producing countries with satisfactory results.

Exports of hops from Austria:

	Quantity.	Value.
	cwts.	florins.
1868	75,034	7,503,400
1869	33,094	3,309,400
1870	43,840	4,384,000

In ROUMANIA the hop is not yet submitted to any system of regular culture, but the wild hops which grow in the woods are collected and used as a legume, and also in the manufacture of beer.

SWEDEN.—The hop grows spontaneously, and has done for centuries in a wild state, in many parts of Sweden, as far as Jemtland, and it is cultivated in Northbothnia (66°), at from 36 to 50 miles from the coast. The most common sorts are an early kind, a late variety, and the best and most sought after a variety with red bine and large reddish-brown cones. Many foreign sorts have, however, been introduced and tried of late years.

HOLLAND.—The following figures give the statistics of hop production in the Netherlands, as far as I have been able to ascertain it:

	Acres.	Yield.
		lbs.
1866	395	979,889
1868	1116	480,569
1869	571	
1870		
1871	435	
1872	470	
1873	518	
1874	474	

BELGIUM.—Although hop cultivation is carried on in six of the provinces of Belgium, there are only a small number of arrondissements where it has attained any real importance. All the arrondissements of Hainault, with the exception of Tournai, cultivate the hop, but in Brabant the culture is almost exclusively restricted to the arrondissement of Brussels, in West Flanders to that of Ypres, in East Flanders to Alost, and in the province of Liege to the district of Liege. Beyond these localities we only meet with insignificant hop grounds, generally for the special wants of the grower.

The Belgian hops of Poperinghe and its neighbourhood, and those of Alost, have a good reputation, but the careless mode of gathering and drying are much complained of. This depreciation in the value might easily be remedied by more care being paid to these essential operations. In 1846 2232 hectares were under culture with hops; in 1870, 3960 hectares, yielding an average of 1237 kilogrammes per hectare.

In 1866 the division for provinces, according to the census, was as follows:

	Hectares.
West Flanders (Poperinghe)	1498
Brabant and its vicinity	1348
East Flanders and its vicinity	493
Hainault	448
Liege	128
Total	3915

The number of acres under hops in English measure was, in 1866, 9781, and the produce of hops 10,801,646 lbs.

The culture is now carried on on a much larger scale, judging by the great increase in the exports. Thirty years ago they only amounted to about 1,200,000 lbs., now they exceed 11,000,000 lbs., and the local consumption of beer has also largely increased. In 1860 the quantity of Belgian hops exported, principally to France, England, and Holland, was only about 2,600,000 lbs., valued at 160,000*l*. In 1865 the exports were 5,570,000 lbs., valued at 243,000*l*., and in 1874 over 11,394,000 lbs., valued at 590,400*l*.

The imports of hops into Belgium were, in 1872, 284 bales; 1873, 167 bales; and 1874, 880 bales. In the latter year 430 bales were received from Great Britain, 440 bales from Hamburg, and 10 from the United States.

The following table shows the countries to which Belgian hops are chiefly imported:

	1860.	1865.
	kilogrammes.	kilogrammes.
France	505,554	914,516
England	373,003	990,535
Holland	131,671	372,560
Prussia	90,458	127,113
Hanse Towns	42,706	94,815
Sweden and Norway ..	16,396	18,753
Denmark	6,945	4,968
Chili	2,910	4,731
Other countries	4,136	2,212
Total	1,173,679	2,550,203

In 1851 Belgium exhibited fair samples of hops, and of several varieties, at the Great Exhibition, which ranked next to the Canadian in point of flavour.

The Mayentz hops were also of good flavour and well harvested, though rather small.

At the various International Exhibitions held since, the Belgian hops exhibited were favourably mentioned.

The following table shows the imports and exports of hops for Belgium for a series of years :

| | Imports. | | Exports. | |
	Quantity.	Value.	Quantity,	Value.
	kilogrammes.	francs.	kilogrammes.	francs.
1860	434,337	652,000	1,173,679	3,991,000
1861	462,301	740,000	2,134,132	5,335,000
1862	1,064,989	1,065,000	1,701,071	3,402,000
1863	908,445	636,000	1,633,466	2,777,000
1864	1,249,285	1,249,000	1,389,498	3,335,000
1865	796,624	796,624	2,530,203	6,072,000
1866	..	1,770,000	..	4,903,000
1867	..	1,912,000	..	11,050,000
1868	2,130,488	2,130,000	1,958,841	2,351,000
1869	2,337,145	2,337,000	2,663,242	3,160,000
1870	1,159,996	698,000	1,462,298	1,020,000
1871	..	3,848,000	..	6,714,000
1872	..	1,305,000	..	5,779,000
1873	1,247,000	1,996,000	4,127,000	7,221,000
1874	1,221,000	2,915,000	5,179,000	14,760,000

Imports of hops, in kilogrammes of 2⅕ lbs. :

From	1868.	1869.	1870.
	kilog.	kilog.	kilog.
United Kingdom	131,656	47,198	65,462
France	1,100,798	1,271,577	452,227
Zollverein	706,124	699,009	434,876
Total	2,130,488	2,337,145	1,159,996

Exports :

To	1868.	1869.	1870.
	kilog.	kilog.	kilog.
United Kingdom	1,121,944	1,766,598	602,055
Holland	340,884	264,801	330,967
France	446,676	514,767	448,938
Total	1,958,841	2,633,242	1,462,298

FRANCE.—The hop is grown in the north of France and the departments of la Somme and Pas-de-Calais.

The hops planted in the department of the Bas Rhine in 1857 covered a superficies of 574 hectares ($2\frac{1}{2}$ acres each), and there were 120 additional hectares planted in the next eight years. In 1845 France imported 721,000 kilos. of hops; in 1855, 1,556,000 kilos.

French brewers for a number of years were accustomed to make beer without hops. They substituted for it coriander seed, wormwood, and the bark of boxwood; but the bad quality of the beer thus made disgusted their customers, and they compelled brewers to use hops as the only substance which can produce a wholesome beverage.

In 1825 every inhabitant in France consumed but nine quarts of beer; in 1837 this had increased to nearly twenty litres, and since then it has progressively increased.

Beer is the popular drink of the departments of the North, Pas-de-Calais, and Ardennes.

In 1859 the quantity of beer made was 6,696,761 hectolitres; in 1866, 8,078,478 hectolitres.

In 1862 there were 11,920 acres under hops, which produced 14,003,514 lbs. The yield per hectare was 1430 kilogrammes (of 2 lbs.), being an increase of 360 kilogrammes of dry cones per hectare over 1840.

Hops occupied in 1871, 4263 hectares, the production being 57,153 cwt., valued at 11,539,126 francs.

In 1872 the acreage under hops was 9223 acres, and the yield of the crop 14,003,514 lbs., or 40,706 cwt., valued at 162 frs. 62 c. the cwt.

This culture is only important in the following departments:

	Cwts.
Nord	23,310
Haute Saone	11,654
Meurthe-et-Moselle	7,662
Côte d'Or	7,300
Aisne	2,870
Vosges	2,002

Thus these six departments produced 54,798 cwt., or 95 per cent. of the whole. There are only thirteen departments in which it is grown. The loss of Alsace and Lorraine caused a considerable reduction, as these departments produced in 1862, 20,500 cwt.

The culture of hops was introduced into Alsace in 1803, by the late M. Charles Ehrenpfort, of Hagueneau. M. Ehrenpfort had to overcome many difficulties, until the hops were at last admitted by the brewers of the country, who, accustomed to the use of German hops, would not use the native-grown. This state of things discouraged the first planters. It was only in 1819 that M. Ehrenpfort succeeded in having his hops brewed in Alsace, by sacrificing several bales of his merchandise, which he managed to get a brewer of Strasburg to take, through the agency at first of a German merchant, and afterwards direct. The first successes obtained, other brewers were encouraged, and the culture of hops gradually developed in Alsace. The best qualities are found at Wissemburg, Molsheim, and Neuviller; and the whole production of Alsace at present amounts to about 40,000 metrical quintals (cwts.) every year.*

* 'Journal de l'Académie Nationale,' 1874, p. 433.

SWITZERLAND.—The following figures give the imports of hops into Switzerland for a series of years:

	Cwts.		Cwts.
1860	2110	1867	3981
1861	3301	1868	4186
1862	3489	1869	4346
1863	3593	1870	4942
1864	3715	1871	5918
1865	4604	1872	5866
1866	4215	1873	7659

CHAPTER VII.

PRODUCTION ON THE AMERICAN CONTINENT.

UNITED STATES.—The hop plant was introduced into the British North American colonies soon after the first European settlements, and cultivated in New Netherlands in 1629, and in Virginia as early as 1648.

In 1840 the United States only produced 6000 bales of hops; ten years later, 1849, the production had increased to 17,000 bales. The next decade showed a larger increase than in any other product, the growth of 1859 reaching 55,000 bales. The crop of 1862 was estimated at 80,000 bales, that of 1863 at 65,000, and of 1864 at 45,000 bales.

In 1845 the hops grown in North America were:

	Bales.
New England States	4250
New York	4000
Total	8250

which was 2000 bales less than the previous year.

Hop culture is now pretty generally diffused over the States; Vermont, New Hampshire, and Massachusetts are the principal New England hop-growing States. According to the census of 1849 the quantity of hops raised in the States was 3,497,029 lbs., of which New England produced 707,743 lbs., New York 2,536,299 lbs., and all the other States only 253,987 lbs.

In 1854 the growth was about 27,000 bales, of 200 lbs. to

the bale, which was beyond the average of previous years by 6000 to 8000 bales. In 1860 the produce of hops, according to the census, was 5844 tons, and the value of the beer used in the States, 3,754,400*l*. At the previous census, 1294 tons of hops were returned, and 1,777,924 barrels of beer made.

Little or no hops were grown in the Southern States. The climate is unfavourable to the growth of the plant; attempts have been recently made to grow it in the mountainous region of South Carolina and Tenessee, but the results have been insignificant. In the State of Kentucky five or six bales were produced in 1873, in the more Northern States, as Illinois, Indiana, and Iowa, a small quantity has been grown. The only States where there is any important production are New York, Wisconsin, Michigan, and California.

The production of hops in the United States, according to the last census of 1870, was 25,456,669 lbs., the principal producing States being the following:

	Lbs.
New York	17,558,681
Wisconsin	4,630,155
California	625,064
Michigan	828,269
Vermont	527,927
Minnesota	222,065
Maine	296,850
Iowa	171,113

New Hampshire, Ohio, and Pennsylvania produce about 100,000 lbs. each.

The crop for the Union in 1874 was estimated as follows:

	Bales.
New York	50,000
Wisconsin	22,000
California	5,000
Michigan	5,000
Other States	15,000
Total	97,000

In Maine there was a heavy yield of hops in 1874. In California hops of good quality are grown in the Sacramento and San José valleys. In 1874 the production amounted to nearly 10,000 cwt., which was sold at from 6*l*. 5*s*. to 7*l*. per cwt., chiefly for shipment to the Eastern States.

The entire consumption of hops in the States is estimated at 125,000 bales, so that about 30,000 bales of foreign hops would be required to meet the demand; but the fact is, the supply from Europe is much larger, because a considerable quantity of American hops is shipped across the Atlantic, where they meet with a sale, owing to their cheaper prices. They may be bought at from 4*d*. to 6*d*. per lb.; while Bavarian hops sell at 7*d*. per lb.

The following figures give the imports of hops into the United States, and their value:

	Lbs.	Dollars.
1861	8,836,000	2,006,053
1862	4,860,000	663,898
1863	8,864,000	1,733,265
1864	5,851,000	1,217,075
1865	3,662,734	1,348,263
1866	350,000	108,752
1867	1,001,603	362,946
1868	532,000	264,129
1869	11,270,000	1,627,248
1870	16,356,000	2,545,734
1871	3,274,000	316,288
1872	3,061,000	408,305
1873	1,795,437	272,403
1874	117,358	27,973

The export of American hops to Europe in 1873 was 20,000 bales, and the brewers of the United States had to buy about 50,000 bales, or nearly two-fifths of their consumption.

The price of hops in New York in January, 1875, was as follows:

	Cents.
First quality	42 to 48 per lb.
Ordinary	35 „ 40 „
Of the East and West	35 „ 40 „
California	45 „ 50 „
1873	15 „ 25 „
1872 and 1871	8 „ 15 „

Cultivation and Preparation in the United States.—The plant is propagated by cuttings of the rhizomes, that are sent out from the main root annually, and have to be removed each year, which constitutes what is termed grubbing. This is performed in the spring, as soon as the frost is out of the ground sufficiently to permit that the young shoot or vine, after it starts, may not be broken off during the process.

In Wisconsin the kind of soil found best adapted to the growth of the plant in the vicinity of Reedsburg, Sauk county, is a rich, black, sandy loam, with a subsoil that will hold water well, enabling the vine to withstand drought.

The locations found to be best adapted are elevated table-lands, where there is a free circulation of air, but shielded from heavy winds, which are very injurious to the fruit at the time of ripening, because these whip the branches against each other, breaking off some and causing the outer surface of the bracts to turn reddish brown, which greatly injures the appearance.

In starting hop fields, the rhizomes removed by grubbing are cut into pieces 6 to 8 inches long, each piece containing two or three pairs of eyes, and planted as early in the spring as the weather will permit, usually in April, four or five pieces being placed in a hill. The hills are usually set

8 feet apart in each direction, and in straight rows. The hop plant does not yield the first year, but only in the second year, when the vine is trained on poles prepared for the purpose, 15 to 16 feet in height; two or three poles are set to a hill, and two or three vines are run up each pole. When three poles are used, generally two vines are run up each.

The plant flowers about the middle of July, and remains in blossom from a week to ten days, when it expands (which is termed hopping out) and forms the strobiles of commerce. They soon attain their full size; but are allowed to remain on the vine to mature until about the 1st of September, when picking commences. The picking is performed mostly by women and children, who gather the fruit into boxes, the size of which is regulated by law. Each consists of a large box, usually made of pine or some light wood, divided into four equal compartments, each compartment measuring 3 feet long, $1\frac{1}{2}$ foot wide, and 2 feet in depth, and holding about 7 bushels.

The pickers are arranged four to a box, each picking in one of the small compartments, which constitutes, when full, what is termed a box of hops. The average number of boxes picked per day by the pickers is two; this varies, however, according to the activity of the person, some picking three to four, and others only one to one and a half boxes. They receive generally from thirty to forty cents per box. The average weight of a box of hops when dried is about 10 lbs. The drying is performed in kilns, in houses which are built either of stone, brick, or wood. Stone or brick is preferred, but wood is mostly used in Wisconsin, and is plastered all the way up on the inside to the peak, to prevent the escape of heated air laterally.

The kilns vary in size. A common size is 16 × 20 feet, and 14 to 15 feet from the ground to the kiln floor, and about 8 feet from the kiln floor to the gable roof, which has an opening or cupola in the centre of the peak. The kiln floor is made of slats 1 inch by 2 or 2½ inches, set upon the edge, about 2 inches apart, upon which is spread a cloth, usually "burlap," coarse linen, weighing 11 ounces to the yard. At the bottom of the kiln, on each side, are one or two holes, about 3 feet long by 1 foot high, called air-holes, and closed by a slide. The heat is received from a stove placed on the ground floor, with the pipe running around the room in the form of a square, or parallel with the walls of the kiln, about 5 or 6 feet below the kiln cloth, so as not to scorch the hops. The hops are now placed upon the kiln, and are spread from a foot to a foot and a half in thickness. The fire is then started gradually, with the air-holes open below, and the cupola open above, to admit a good current of cool air coming in from below, and allow the escape of the heated air from the top. The temperature is raised during the early part of the drying to 100°–120° Fahr., when the hops have become thoroughly warmed, so as to give out their moisture, which is commonly known as sweating. Brimstone is burnt on the stove for the purpose of bleaching. The quantity of brimstone used varies according to the condition of the hop; when the hop is bright and free from disease, and a light green colour is desired, only two or three pounds are used to a kiln of about twenty boxes; but when a bright golden-yellow colour is required, or when the hop has been injured by disease or wind, then larger quantities are necessary, say from three to four pounds, or even as high as five or six pounds. The brimstone is placed in a little dish on the stove, a small quantity at a time, and this is repeated until the moisture is mostly expelled from the hop. In some instances, when the hop has been injured, or become brown on the vine, the bleaching process is desired to be continued after the natural moisture has been expelled. In this case sprinkling the hop on the kiln, or setting kettles of water on the stove, are resorted to. The time required to dry a kiln of hops is about twelve hours. When the hop is a little green, as at the beginning of the picking season, more time is required; and at the close, when the hop has become fully ripe and does not contain as much moisture, less time is required. The heat should be very carefully regulated, not running above 100° or 120° Fahr. in the commencement, as there is danger of scorching when the hop is full of moisture, then gradually increasing the heat, as the process goes on, to 140°–150° Fahr. Great care is necessary, that the temperature is not allowed to recede during any stage of the process, as the steam will settle back on the hops and give them a dull, darkish colour, which materially lessens their market value. The drying is considered complete when one hop out of four or five is found brittle as taken from the surface of different parts of the kiln. The fires are then suffered to die out, and the hops allowed to remain on the kiln until cool, the doors being thrown open to hasten the cooling. They are then removed from the kiln into a room, called a cooling room, where they are allowed to lie until wanted for baling. They ought to be examined every day to see that they do not heat, which is sometimes the case when insufficiently dried. They should be allowed to remain in the cooling room four or five days before baling, or better, about two weeks, when not in haste to place them on the market, as they are not then required to be dried quite so much on the kiln, and allowed to finish in the cooling room, which makes a softer, silkier sample, and one not as liable to be broken and powdered in baling.

Baling is performed in portable presses of sufficient power to make a handsome bale, weighing about 200 lbs. Care is necessary in baling not to powder and break the hops, as there is a great loss of strength by the lupuline sifting out, and it also injures the appearance, upon which their market value largely depends.

In the years of 1866-68 the yield reached the almost incredible amount of 2400 to 2500 lbs. per acre, 2000 lbs. being considered a fair yield. Since then, owing partly to a lack of care in culture, caused by a decline in price for a few years below the cost of production, and the presence in the fields of the hop-leaf louse (*Aphis humulus*), the average has fallen; this insect appears on the lower leaves of the vine about the middle or end of June. When the weather is favourable (warm, muggy weather especially), they increase so rapidly that they weaken the vine by sapping the juice; they do not do much damage usually until the hop is fully formed and a few days before picking, when, if the weather is hot and close, two or three days are sufficient to almost destroy the whole crop. They penetrate the hop after it is formed and suck the juice from the tender bracts, and this piercing causes the juice to exude, which, in dry or bright weather, evaporates and does no damage; but in damp, muggy weather the evaporation is so retarded that it produces decay at the point of puncture, the effect of which is a black spot, known as mould; and, when the lice are in sufficient numbers, the strobiles will be found to be almost entirely black inside, and are then nearly worthless. This and other causes have lessened the vitality of the vine to such an extent, that 1200 to 1500 lbs. per acre is now a large yield, and the average yield will not exceed 600 to 800 lbs. per acre. The crop of the entire State of Wisconsin for 1874 was from 17,000 to 20,000 bales, not over about one-half what it was in 1868. The cultivation of hops is, however, allowed to be more remunerative than any other class of farming, when followed for a succession of years.

CANADA.—Before 1852 Canada did not grow enough hops for her own consumption, for she imported 37,653 lbs. in 1850, and 16,694 lbs. in 1851. The growth in 1852 was but 224,222 lbs. The frosts there frequently kill the plants. It was only in 1848 that hops began to be exported, 42,978 lbs. having been shipped in that year.

In 1849 the shipments were 24,687 lbs. and nine packs, valued at 387*l*. The following have been the shipments from Canada for some few other years:

	Lbs.	Value.
		£
1850	29,182	540
1851	72,223	1,579
1852	47,683	1,314
1853	8,741	378
1854	165,868	8,370
1868	220,457	72,677
1869	411,842	46,898
1870	..	..
1873	..	320,286

BRAZIL.—Until a few years ago all the hops consumed in Brazil were imported; but on account of the increase of home-made ale, the colony of San Leopoldo, in the province of Rio Grande de Sud, commenced its cultivation about ten years ago, and, favoured by the climate and the nature of the soil, it promises to succeed and to make progress, for the imported hops are not only injured by the sea voyage, but fetch a high price. Samples of the Brazilian hops were shown at the Paris International Exhibition in 1867.

CHAPTER VIII.

HOP CULTURE IN AUSTRALASIA.

TASMANIA.—New Norfolk and the adjacent districts are well known as the principal hop-growing portions of Tasmania. In the immediate vicinity of the town are numerous grounds, located on strips and flats of rich alluvial ground, both on the banks of the Derwent and those of the Lachlan. On the latter dams are made, and the soil irrigated by gravitation. On the Derwent it is generally necessary to pump the water from the river, and this is effected by steam-engines; for though windmills have been tried, they have been given up, owing to the caprice of the winds, which frequently fail to blow, when water is indispensable. In the town and its immediate vicinity Mr. Riddoch cultivates about 14 acres of hops; Mr. Turnbull, 15 acres; Mr. Allwright has about 16 acres on the Lachlan Creek; Mr. Terry, of Lachlan Mills, 13 acres; Mr. Sharland, 12 acres, in different patches; Mr. Downie, near the bridge, about 9 acres; Sir Robert Officer, about 6 acres. Mr. William Davis has about 5 acres on the Lachlan Creek; Mr. W. E. Shoobridge, 20 acres; at a greater distance, Mr. E. Shoobridge, the largest grower in the island, has upwards of 90 acres planted, 78 acres in full bearing; Mr. R. C. Read, of Redland, the second largest grower, has 24 acres in bearing, and 16 more planted. The area occupied by smaller growers is estimated to amount to somewhere about 256 acres, making a total of 468 acres; in addition to which Mr. S. P. H. Wright cultivates somewhere about 20 acres lower down the Derwent, at O'Brien's Bridge. On the Huon River a large area has been planted, and is now in bearing; so that, although it has been reduced in some districts, the total area under hop culture in the island must show an increase over that of last year, given in the Government statistics at 664 acres of all ages, which produced 825,306 lbs. from 627 acres in bearing, equal to a little over 1300 lbs., or about $11\frac{3}{4}$ cwt. per acre; considering that some of the plantations were not at maturity and others imperfectly cultivated, this may be taken as a fair crop, though in the New Norfolk district the yield was upwards of 13 cwt. per acre.

Irrigation is almost universally practised, there being very few soils on which hops can be successfully grown without artificial watering. But in a few situations it can be done; for instance, where the land lies low, with a porous subsoil, and near to a river or at the foot of a hill, where the subsoil is kept moist by soakage. To derive the greatest amount of benefit from irrigation both scientific knowledge and experience are necessary, so that water may be given at the proper time and in the proper quantity, any excess or deficiency giving a check to the plants and encouraging the increase of the red spider, which appears to be always present and ready to multiply and increase, to the injury and sometimes total destruction of the hops. Instances are given where grounds over-irrigated have suffered to a serious extent, while portions of the same, lying above the reach of the water, were not at all affected. Though the climate is exceedingly favourable for the culture of the hop, the mean diurnal range for the first four months of the year being only 18°, yet a cold night occasionally occurs; and should the ground at that time be fully irrigated, the flow of sap is sure to be arrested and stagnation produced, causing a condition of foliage favourable to the development and increase of the spider. *Sulphuring has been tried as a remedy, but without success, though whether the experiments were carried out to a reasonable extent is doubtful. The usual plan is to gather the hops as soon as possible from the infested plants, and by destroying the plants preventing the insects from spreading. It is highly important that irrigation should be commenced in time, before the natural moisture of the soil is exhausted; and it is of equal importance to leave off at the right time, though occasionally the water is let on to plants not quite ripe, in order to keep them green, when pickers are scarce. The common method of poling is still all but universally prevalent, though Coley's plan has been tried by Sir R. Officer and a few others, and liked by all; but the greater expense in the first instance is acting as a deterrent, and permits but a very slow extension. Manuring is another very important element in the attainment of success, for without an abundance of manure of some kind hops cannot at all be grown successfully for more than a few years, even on the richest soil.

Mr. S. P. H. Wright has a very promising and well-managed hop ground, in a well-chosen situation on the banks of the Derwent, and close to the main road from Hobart Town. A creek flows through the ground, and supplies water for irrigation. The total area of the ground is 34 acres;

about five acres is in orchard and garden, and a large portion of the remainder planted with hops of different ages. The ground is quite flat, and therefore well adapted for irrigation. Rows of poplars and willows have been planted around for shelter, as the winds from the mountains are occasionally very violent. Several acres of ground have been reclaimed from the river, and, like the rest of the soil, proves of excellent quality, as shown by the weeds upon portions not yet planted, which are of immense size. In consequence of the saltness of the water, it is found necessary to let the reclaimed land lie fallow for a year, until a portion of the salt is washed out of it; some of the willows that were planted as breakwinds having failed from the excess of salt in the soil. The varieties of hops grown are Goldings and Grapes. They are planted 6 to 8 feet apart, one male to fifty females, though occasionally a bi-sexual plant (producing both male and female blossoms) is to be seen. They arrive at maturity the third year after planting. Three poles are placed to each hill, their cost being 14s. per 100; 100,000 are on the ground, and, as they rarely last longer than three years, form a very heavy item of expenditure. Creosote has been hitherto used for preserving the ends of the poles, but it is found to be too expensive; and probably the ordinary plan of dipping in boiling coal-tar will in future be followed. A small portion has been poled on Coley's principle, which has given entire satisfaction, and though much more expensive in the beginning, costing 60l. per acre, is likely to prove economical in the long run. Mr. Wright has simplified the plan by making notches in the tops of the upright poles, instead of lashing two pieces of wire to each to receive the tops of the sloping poles. The present year's crop is very good, and the hops are of excellent quality. The Grapes produce a much greater weight than the Goldings, but the latter being finer in quality, bring a higher price in the market. The pickers are paid $1\frac{1}{2}d.$ per bushel, and a woman who is a good hand can pick about 15 bushels per day. The season lasts five or six weeks, and the money earned by the number of poor families who assemble from Hobart Town and the neighbourhood conduces greatly to the comfort during the following winter of those who are sufficiently provident to make a proper use of it. But the sparseness of the population is very likely to prove a hindrance to the increase of hop growing, as already the growers are complaining of the shortness of hands; for if the hops are not picked directly they are ready, deterioration in quality rapidly ensues; and as hop merchants are very fastidious in regard to quality, the slightest injury to the sample, from discoloration or any other cause, brings down the price at an apparently disproportionate rate.

To show the extent to which hop growing is carried on, it may be added that in the New Norfolk and Hobart Town districts there are some 2500 persons, chiefly women and children, employed in picking. All these earn from 4s. to 5s. per day, at the prices paid by the proprietors of the hop grounds.

Mr. Wright has receiving rooms, pressing rooms, and storerooms; and has erected an excellent kiln for drying, holding 500 bushels of green hops, which, when dry, fill three bales of $2\frac{1}{2}$ cwt. each. The hops require twelve hours to dry, and are once turned in the time. The heat is derived from charcoal and anthracite, both obtained within a short distance.

As the hops must not be allowed to lie more than a few hours after being gathered until they are placed on the kiln, exact arrangements require to be made to keep the different operations of picking, drying, and pressing all going on at the same rate. This is admirably managed by Mr. Wright's two sons, who conduct the work in an energetic and business-like manner; and, although refined and educated gentlemen, they not only superintend the work, but do not hesitate to put their hands to even the heaviest portions—one looking after the picking, and the other attending to the drying, packing, &c., one or other being on the spot night and day throughout the season. Stable and other kinds of manure are used for the ground, but Mr. White gives the preference to superphosphate of lime.

It would be difficult to over-estimate the value of this industry to the colony. As a means of employing labour alone it is invaluable. Hop growing is now one, indeed, is the most promising of Tasmanian industries, and regarded as a most remunerative employment.

At the Lackland Cot estate, belonging to Mr. Allwright, the kiln for the drying of hops is a room about 20 feet square, having an air chimney in the centre of the roof; the floor is constructed on the batten principle, rafters of hard wood being placed parallel with each other, with an inch space left between them. This floor is covered with a coarse hair-cloth, which lets the heat through, and upon this the hops are dried. In the room below the kiln is a large square furnace, with four fires, one in each face, and above this is what is called the fire-room or conductor; a closely bricked partition rising from the furnace on either side, to the edge of the ceiling, and so enclosing the heat below the floor of the kiln. After being placed in the kiln the hops are turned with a wooden rake, and are dried until the leaves become brittle, and rub off easily. They are then removed to the cooling room, which is a large apartment under the same roof, 50 feet long, where they are laid in heaps, ready for packing or bagging. The plan adopted for packing hops is the same as that by which wool in the neighbouring colonies is packed, and the ordinary screw press, which is used for this purpose, communicates with the apartment below, which is the storing room. The hop pack is placed in the box, as in the case of wool, and the hops are then thrown in through the aperture in the floor of the upper apartment, and when this is full the screw descends, and the whole are pressed tightly into the pack. Before the hops are baled, they are passed through a coarse sieve of cane, which breaks them up thoroughly, and also removes any portion of the vine stalk which may accidentally have been overlooked in measuring. Mr. Allwright has every convenience attached to his kiln, and he expects it to answer his purpose admirably.

At New Norfolk, the oldest hop-growing district, the average per acre increased from 607·96 lbs. in 1868–9 to 837·45 lbs. in 1869–70; in the district of Hobart it increased from 148 lbs. to 611·94 lbs.; at Brighton, from 250 lbs. to 400 lbs.; at Glenorchy, from 154·80 lbs. to 451·61 lbs.; and so with other districts. The gross yield increased from 242·268 lbs. to 415·064 lbs., or 71·32 per cent.

There are now fourteen districts in the island in which hops are grown.

In the Huon district hop growing has been established, and with the best prospects. There are many other localities equally favourably situated for the cultivation of this crop. The yield in New Norfolk in 1866 was 45 tons; in 1867 it had increased to 70 tons; in 1868, 100 tons; and in 1869, 100 tons, which fetched from 1s. to 2s. per pound.

A return of the hops grown in the district of New Norfolk, published in the 'Hobart Town Mercury' for 1870, showed that there were seventy hop growers, with 447 acres under culture. The produce amounted to 166 tons 16 cwt. 1 qr. 20 lbs. It will be the hop growers' own fault if Tasmania does not soon supply all Australia and New Zealand, if not entirely, yet mainly.

Among the remedies which have been tried to destroy the red spider which has played such havoc among the hops during past seasons, are sulphur, dilute decoction of tobacco, and carbolic acid. Dr. Turnley is of opinion that a gallon of the common acid, to about two or three hundred of water, would be found strong enough for the object required. It is yet a debatable point whether the dilution could be applied without injury to the plant itself, or its marketable product. Dr. Agnew, after making a microscopical examination of the red spider, gave it as his opinion that the insect was identical with the *Acarus telarius*, as figured in McIntosh's 'Book of the Garden,' vol. ii. p. 77; although a later authority gave it the name of *Gamasus telarius*, an allied genus of the same great class, *Arachnida*. It is oviparous, and many broods are hatched during the season. The ova are probably for the most part deposited on the under surface of the leaves, whence the young when hatched can extract nourishment;

but it is possible some may also be deposited in the bark of the hop poles, or even in the ground, where the animals themselves are found in great numbers. The presence of the pest is attempted to be accounted for in two ways. Some think the hop itself, from exposure to high winds, from scant supply of water or manure, or from other causes, first becomes sickly, and thus favours or provokes the development of the spider. Others think the fault is not in the plant in the first instance; but that under some peculiar and unknown influence, whether atmospheric or telluric, or by consent of both, vast developments of animal life take place at certain periods, in a manner not yet accounted for. As to remedial measures, every suitable hygienic application should be adopted, and due shelter from winds afforded. If the ground is found to be exhausted of any necessary chemical element, this should be restored, and proper quantities of manure and water furnished. From the numbers of the insects found in the bark, it is evident the poles should be carefully deprived of their bark, and it would probably be advisable to soak them in tar before setting them up.

VICTORIA.—In the second Progress Report of a Royal Commission appointed in Victoria to inquire how far it might be practicable to introduce into that colony branches of industry known to be common and profitable among the farming population of continental Europe, published in 1872, I find the following passage on this subject:

"Although hop growing may be neither a novel nor a foreign industry, it has been considered by us as one of great importance, and has commanded our attention. The first planters of hops in this colony were not acquainted with the practices elsewhere, and printed instructions were not easily to be had, if we except the few articles on this subject which have appeared in the weekly papers from time to time. Thus the pioneers in this branch of rural industry have had to acquire experimentally, as it were, their knowledge; but they have proved parts of the colony to be eminently adapted for the growth of hops. Labour was scarce and dear at picking time, and the oasting part of the work was not understood, so that the pecuniary returns were at first disappointing; but experience has convinced the growers that further knowledge is alone required to render their hop gardens highly remunerative. To supply this in part Mr. Howitt obtained from Kent plans of the most approved kilns or oasts, which he kindly placed at the disposal of the Commission. And it may be encouraging to say that in Gippsland very simple kilns have been erected of rough materials and at moderate cost, with which complete success has been achieved. But this result was not obtained by the means before alluded to, but by the skill of an experienced hop-curer, who was engaged at other work, until he learned from the published reports of our proceedings that practical knowledge of the kind was needed by the growers of hops in a part of the country with which he was not previously acquainted."

Wherever beer is made hops form a serious item of expenditure, and it is probable that within a few years enough may be grown in Victoria to supply the demands of the colony, even if they were not readily obtainable in Tasmania. Hop gardens have been made in Gippsland and in the Ovens district, and the plant tried successfully in other parts of the colony. Of the prospects of this branch of agricultural industry in North Gippsland, a settler near Bairnsdale thus speaks:

"The writer has expended a large sum of money in hop growing; soil and climate admirably adapted, but labour scarce and dear at picking time. With cheap labour this industry may be extended almost indefinitely in the valley of the Mitchell. Hop plants two years old produced last year (1872) 11 cwt. to the acre, and upwards, within half a mile of Bairnsdale."

Did space allow, I could add the testimony of many other growers of hops in Gippsland. A gentleman residing near Raley writes to say that he has 11 acres of hops, which will be in full bearing this year, and look very promising. These have since yielded upwards of half a ton to the acre. The only difficulty experienced in Gippsland was the picking and drying; but proper kilns have now been erected, and as properly cured colonial hops always fetch the highest prices, they will admit for a time of a somewhat extra cost for picking.

This twining perennial unisexual plant has been found to yield enormously on river banks in Victoria, in rich soil, or on fertile slopes where irrigation could be effected, particularly so within the territory along the river valleys of Gippsland, and other similar localities. A pervious, especially alluvial soil, fertile through manure or otherwise, appliances for irrigation, natural or artificial, and also shelter against storms, are some of the conditions for success in hop growth, and under such conditions the rearing of hops will prove thus far profitable in countries and localities of very different mean temperature. A dry summer season is favourable to the ripening and gathering of hops. On the Mitchell River, in Gippsland, 1500 lbs. have been obtained from an acre. The plant might be readily naturalized on river banks and in forest valleys.*

We find, then, that in this colony the hop grows in the greatest perfection. Of it a resident of North Gippsland says, in the official colonial 'Report on Novel Industries': "In reference to hops, which I cultivate, I sustained considerable loss last season from not having the necessary skill in drying and sowing, and having no books on the subject to which I could refer. With reference to my experience of their culture, I regard them as an unqualified success, pronounced by persons able to judge as being equal in one year to a crop planted three years in England; and as a proof of their extraordinary growth, I may mention that they require poles several feet higher here. The varieties I cultivate are the Grape and the Golding. This year I have extended my plantation, and purpose extending it as my means permit." The opinions of many cultivators of this plant in Gippsland were furnished to the Royal Commission, and all agreed in saying that the hop is most easily reared, subject to no diseases as yet, and bears abundantly at an early date. But all the growers have suffered more or less from the want of knowledge in drying the hops and preparing them for market.

In Victoria the production of hops was as follows:

	1874.	1875.
Acreage	131	126
Pounds produced	83,328	99,624

* Baron Mueller, on "Select Plants readily eligible for Victorian Industrial Culture."

In 1854 the beer brewed in Victoria was 1,366,165 gallons, or 4¾ gallons per head of the population.

In 1864 there were 74 breweries in Victoria, employing 495 persons, in which upwards of 4,000,000 gallons of beer were brewed during the year.

The official statistics of the colony of Victoria give the following details respecting breweries in 1875:

Total number	107
Hands employed	925
Horses employed	663
Drays and waggons	364
Sugar used, lbs.	8,816,864
Malt used, bushels	670,928
Hops used, lbs.	988,863
Beer made, gallons	13,653,531
Value of machinery and plant	£159,313
Value of lands	£65,846
Value of buildings	£211,784

The return, as compared with those made five years previously, shows a falling off in nearly all the items.

It is believed that the truth is understated in respect to the quantity of the different descriptions of material used, and of beer made.

Quantities and value of hops imported into the colony of Victoria:

	£			£
1860	26,450		1864	52,729
1861	34,364		1865	48,179
1862	42,041		1866	70,263
1863	63,839			

	Lbs.			Lbs.
1867	358,939		1870	644,717
1868	583,343		1871	241,387

There is a duty of 2*d.* a pound on hops imported into the colony.

SOUTH AUSTRALIA.—Proofs of the successful growth of hops in South Australia are shown in the samples exhibited by Sir T. Kleinschmidt, of Lobethal, Mr. Bell, of Encounter Bay, and at Mount Barker, at the Exhibitions. It is true that there are not many favourable districts in the colony for the profitable growth of this valuable plant; but there is no doubt that in other districts besides the above named, suitable spots will be found. Dr. Schomburgk, the Colonial botanist, has tried ineffectually several years to introduce the male plant, which in a hop plantation is considered valuable for the production of seed, as it improves the flavour materially.

NEW ZEALAND.—Hops are grown successfully in the province of Nelson. There is a rather extensive hop ground near the city of Nelson.

The Nelson hop crop (1875) is thus spoken of in a recent number of the 'Colonist': "We have much pleasure in publishing the following statistics of hop cultivation in the Takaka district, supplied to us by an esteemed correspondent. The writer adds: 'Notwithstanding the gardens in this district are only two years old, the plants have been wonderfully productive. The soil on the banks of the rivers is found to be very suitable for its cultivation, being of great depth, and of an alluvial formation.' Mr. James Spittal, Lower Anatoki, $2\frac{1}{2}$ acres, 4480 lbs.; Mr. James Bridger, Takaka River, $1\frac{1}{4}$ acre, 3551 lbs.; Mr. James Reily, Waitapu, 2 acres, 4480 lbs.; Mr. Francis Y. Hicks, Motupipi River, $\frac{1}{4}$ acre, 500 lbs.; Mr. Alexander M'Farlane, Anatoki, $\frac{1}{2}$ acre, 1120 lbs.; Mr. Alfred Dodson, Long Plain Road, $\frac{1}{4}$ acre, 500 lbs.; Mr. Edward Plummer, Upper Takaka, $\frac{1}{2}$ acre, 1120 lbs."

In the province of Otago hops grow very freely, and produce an abundant crop; whilst the steadily increasing demand and the prices ruling are great inducements to holders of land in favourable localities to grow shelter to protect the vine from the gusts of wind which prevail during summer. It will take some years to produce a supply sufficient for the provincial trade; meanwhile the introduction of a few hands acquainted with the growing, handling, and drying of this valuable plant would be advisable.

The brewing of this province is in high repute, and although at present of large dimensions, it is not sufficient for the home trade and exportation. Dunedin is the principal centre of this business, six extensive establishments being in full work, and an additional one in course of erection. The estimate of the aggregate production is over 1500 hogsheads per month.*

There are two patches of hops cultivated in Taranaki, of a few acres in extent; one in its fourth and the other in its third year of plantation. These thrive well, and yield good returns. The soil and climate seem to suit the hop admirably, and growing them on a large scale would prove a lucrative speculation.

Cultivation in India.

The Indian Government having resolved to seek tenders for a supply of country beer to the large military cantonments of Upper India, it becomes a question of urgent importance as to how far it is possible to naturalize the hop plant on the slopes and in the valleys of the Himalayas.

* 'Official Handbook of New Zealand.'

The first attempt to introduce hop culture in Cashmere was made by Captain (now Colonel) Montgomery, of the Trigonometrical Survey. His hop garden was of very humble dimensions; but the plant thrived satisfactorily, and flowered regularly even after he had quitted Srinuggur. The flower and quality of these hops were pronounced excellent by the manager of the Murree Company, who had obtained a small sack of them; the only deficiency he observed was that they were wanting in the pollen or yellow dust, which is supposed to be an important ingredient of the genuine Kentish brew. It was suspected that the pollen had evaporated through solar exposure, and to ensure its retention kiln drying will therefore have to be employed. The encouraging success attendant upon Colonel Montgomery's trial hop garden induced Mr. Whymper, manager of the above Brewery Company, to start the experimental gardens referred to.

The experiment of growing hops on a sufficiently large scale is now being tried at Srinuggur, on three separate localities in the Cashmere valley, the exceptionally temperate climate of which renders it highly suitable to the growth of the plant. Operations were commenced early in the spring of last year. About six hundred roots were planted in a plot at Srinuggur, obtained by favour of the Maharajah, and a quarter of these are reported to be in a thriving condition, and are already breaking into flower. Another plot, of larger extent, comprising some twelve acres, has also been planted; but the soil is unfavourable, being low and swampy. For this garden 60,000 roots were despatched from England early in the year, and arrived at their destination in

May. But the heat and rough usage of the journey proved fatal to the greater number, and the English superintendent has stated that only about 15,000 were alive when taken out of the sacks. These have been planted with great care, and a large percentage of them gives promise of survival, to repay the very heavy cost already incurred in the experiment. Other experiments are being carried on by Mr. Beck, the local agent for the company, in other parts of Cashmere, by which thousands of plants will be ready for transplanting early next spring.

Hops are as yet but of small importance as an article of import, though they are steadily increasing in demand. The value of the imports of the last four years, as given in the official returns for India, were as follows:

	£		£
1872	5198	1874	8940
1873	5020	1875	11,828

Beer of fair quality is now made in some Indian hill stations, and is coming into extended use among civil residents and the troops in the hills. On the plains, the cost of carriage from the hills prevents this beer competing with imported beer. This country beer is all made of imported hops, attempts to grow hops in the neighbourhood of Simla and other parts of the hills having as yet been unsuccessful.

Hops would seem even to be grown in the Chinese empire, for in 1874, 550 piculs (133 lbs.) were shipped from the port of Chefoo.

CHAPTER IX.

HOP SUBSTITUTES—IMPORTS AND PRICES OF FOREIGN HOPS—
BEER STATISTICS AND MALT CONSUMPTION.

THE superiority of the hop as an ingredient in our malt liquors depends upon the fact of its containing within itself several distinct and independent elements of activity, which the bitter herbs that have at different times been employed as a substitute do not possess.

Professor Dragendorff, the eminent toxicologist of the University of Dorpat, has published in the 'Archiv der Pharmacie of Jena' for 1874, a most valuable paper on his researches into the nature of the bitter substances used in the brewing of beer. This has been translated from the German into French, by our mutual friend Dr. Jules Morel, Professor of Chemistry at Ghent, under the title of 'Sur la Recherche des Substances amères dans la Bière,'* 60 pages; but I am not aware that it has yet appeared in English. It gives practical and complete tests, from large experience, for determining the various adulterants that may possibly be used by the brewer.

The use of hops for beer does not date very far back, as Bazile Valentin is the first author of the middle ages who notices their use; and it was in 1524 that the cultivation was first commenced in Flanders. From that country they were transported to England in the reign of Henry VIII., and soon spread over the counties of Kent, Essex, and Sussex. English hops well prepared, and especially well

* Bruxelles: Jules Combes, 1874.

packed, soon acquired a high reputation. Then Germany and Austria took up the culture, and by careful selection obtained pure and delicate flavoured plants.

Now there are many principal varieties, as has already been indicated.

Among the bitter and tonic substances which have been used as substitutes for hops are the bark of some species of pine and willow, cascarilla bark, quassia, gentian, colocynth, walnut leaf, wormwood bitter, cloves, extract of aloes, cocculus indicus berries, colocynth seeds, capsicum, belladonna, nux vomica, *Ledum palustre*, box leaves, *Menyanthes trifoliata*, *Cnicus benedictus*, *Erythræa Centaurium*, ground ivy, *Daphne Mezereum*, &c.; recently picric acid has been employed. Although all these substances impart a bitter taste to beer, they are inferior to hops. Many of them contain the same constituents, namely, tannic acid, a resin, a bitter extractive, and an essential oil.

Cascarilla bark, used as a tonic, has very wholesome qualities, a pleasant and strong bitterness, and was for some time held in considerable repute among the faculty. About half a century ago large shipments were made from the Bahamas. It was found upon adulteration with hops to reduce the cost of that article, and for the encouragement of the hop growers a prohibitory import duty was laid upon it by the Home Government; consequently it became an unsaleable product.

The list of the principal adulterants, with their scientific names, would seem to be as follows:

Quassia wood	*Quassia amara, Simaruba officinalis.*
Wild Rosemary	*Ledum palustre.*
Wormwood or Absinthe..	{ *Artemisia absinthium, A. mutellina,* and *A. spicata.*
Water Trefoil	*Menyanthes trifoliata.*

Blessed Thistle	*Cnicus benedictus.*
Lesser Centaury	*Erythræa Centaurium.*
Gentian	*Gentiana lutea, amarilla,* &c.
Willow bark	*Salix alba.*
Aloes extract	*Aloe sp.*
Picric acid	
Colocynth	*Cucumis Colocynthis.*
Seeds of Cocculus indicus	*Anamirta paniculata.*
Meadow Saffron	*Colchicum autumnale.*
Bark of	*Daphne Mezereum.*
Fruit of Chillies	*Capsicum annuum.*
Deadly Nightshade leaves	*Atropa Belladonna.*
Henbane leaves	*Hyoscyamus niger.*
Seeds of Nux vomica	*Strychnos Nux vomica.*
Cascarilla bark	*Croton Cascarilla,* and *C. eleuteria.*
Roots of	*Caryophyllata (Geum) lutea.*
Grains of Paradise, seeds of	*Amomum Grana Paradisa.*
Chiretta, the plant	*Agathotis Chirayta.*
Camomile, flowers of	*Anthemis nobilis.*
Alehoof, or ground ivy	*Hedera terrestris.*

In the United States, *Gentiana quinqueflora,* under the names of Indian quinine and ague weed, and *G. saponaria,* are esteemed fully equal to the imported gentian. *Sabbatea angularis,* the American Centaury, *Sab. stellaris,* and *S. gracilis* possess properties similar to the former.

This genus of North American plants is closely allied to Erythræa, of which several species, *E. Chilensis, Centaurium, linarifolia,* &c., are still employed in different countries as tonics.

Stanislaus Martin states that there are met with occasionally in French commerce hops deprived of the principal part of their lupuline by means of sifting, thus keeping back the active principle, the inert cones being sold to pharmaciens and herbalists.*

A year or two ago an important and influential meeting of

* 'Houblon Officinal, son altération.' Bull. de Therap., t. xlvii. p. 288.

gentlemen connected with the hop trade was held at Maidstone, to take into consideration what steps should be taken to check the use of deleterious articles as substitutes for hops in the manufacture of beer. The result of the meeting was that a large and influential committee, consisting of the chief hop growers in the county of Kent, and many hop merchants and factors of the Borough, was appointed, with instructions to form a deputation to wait upon the President of the Board of Trade, or take any other steps which might be deemed necessary with a view to prevent the use of deleterious mixtures as a substitute for hops in the manufacture of beer.

For the reference of those who desire to investigate the subject of hops more fully and minutely than it has been here treated, I may state that there will be found in the volumes of the 'Journal of the Royal Agricultural Society of England' various analyses, as, for instance, by J. C. Nisbet, on the mineral ingredients of the hop, and on the composition of the Golding and yellow Grape hops, vol. vii. p. 210-15; on the analysis of the flower, ix. p. 144, and xiii. p. 474, by Way and Ogsten, xi. p. 514; and of brewers' spent hops, xiii. p. 498. Mr. S. Rutley has also a prize essay on the best mode of managing a hop plantation, vol. ix. p. 532.

Finally, I bring this work to a conclusion with some statistics which may be found useful for reference.

A few figures regarding the highest and lowest scale of duties for a series of years may not be uninteresting, or without use.

From 1712 to 1750 the duty varied from 6,526*l*. in 1725 to 91,880*l*. in 1746
„ 1751 „ 1800 „ „ 14,895*l*. „ 1782 „ 203,663*l*. „ 1794
„ 1801 „ 1850 „ „ 15,463*l*. „ 1802 „ 269,331*l*. „ 1826
„ 1851 „ 1859 „ „ 47,369*l*. „ 1854 „ 398,635*l*. „ 1852
In 1859 the duty was 328,070*l*.

The dates of the occasions when the payment of the duty on hops was deferred were: 1820, 1821, 1822, 1823, 1824, 1827, 1828, 1829, 1831, 1849, 1850, 1857, and 1858.

The seasons of 1855 and 1856 were conspicuous in the history of the hop trade, the former having produced the largest crop on record (over 83 million pounds), and the latter having presented the somewhat unusual phenomenon of a very considerable produce immediately following so extraordinary a luxuriance of growth. The duty in 1855 was no less than 728,183*l*., or almost double the average of years. Prices were of course depressed by this excess of production. Four consecutive years of large produce, 1856 to 1859, necessarily brought down still further the price of hops, and they were sold in the market at rates which, inclusive of the duty, were for the most part unremunerative, and pressing applications were made by the hop planters of the kingdom, some 6500, for the postponement of the payment of the duty, and facilities for payment were granted from time to time by the Chancellor of the Exchequer.

In 1603 several statutes and regulations were made for the curing of hops, which had to be carried out under the inspection of the officers of Excise.

In 1710 a duty of 3*d*. per pound was imposed on all hops imported into England, and in 1734 a duty of 1*d*. per pound was imposed on all grown in this country, which in 1805 was fixed at 2*d*. per pound, subject to a drawback of 10 per cent. in favour of the grower.

In 1840 a further duty of 5 per cent. was imposed upon the whole of the previous charge; the actual duty being thereby raised to 17*s*. 7½*d*. per cwt. On imported hops, until the passing of the tariff of 1842, the duty was 8*l*. 8*s*., a rate which amounted to a virtual prohibition on importation; previous to 1846 it was 4*l*. 5*s*., and then reduced to 2*l*. 5*s*. per cwt. Now abolished.

The duty on foreign hops was reduced from 1*l*. per cwt. to 15*s*. on the 1st of January, 1862, and soon after abolished, and this has led to a large importation.

IMPORTS OF FOREIGN HOPS.

	Cwts.		Cwts.		Cwts.
1840	107	1852	309	1864	98,656
1841	34	1853	43,344	1865	82,479
1842	..	1854	119,040	1866	85,687
1843	28	1855	24,662	1867	296,117
1844	267	1856	15,987	1868	231,720
1845	726	1857	18,711	1869	322,515
1846	3,283	1858	13,000	1870	127,853
1847	1,471	1859	2,220	1871	218,664
1848	385	1860	68,918	1872	135,965
1849	5,265	1861	149,176	1873	122,729
1850	6,479	1862	133,791	1874	145,994
1851	462	1863	147,281	1875	256,444

The average prices fixed by the Board of Trade for the computed real value of the foreign hops imported have been as follows:

	Hanse Towns.			Holland and Belgium.			United States.		
	£	*s.*	*d.*	£	*s.*	*d.*	£	*s.*	*d.*
1855	6	18	0	8	15	0	6	3	0
1860	10	14	2	8	16	0	6	19	6
1861	4	3	10	4	2	6	4	17	2
1862	6	1	6	4	18	5	5	0	5
1863	4	15	1	4	1	0	3	18	3
1864	5	17	0	5	6	7	5	12	3
1865	5	12	4	5	1	6	5	14	2
1866	6	14	10	6	3	6	7	15	3
1867	5	6	3	5	4	8	8	18	10
1868	3	1	6	2	16	2	3	19	0
1869	2	19	0	3	10	4	3	13	0
1870	3	7	0	2	19	0	3	14	0

In 1855 we exported 8904 cwt. of hops of British growth and 12,196 cwt. of foreign growth.
In the last few years the exports have been as follows:

	British.	Foreign.
	cwts.	cwts.
1866	22,864	13,224
1867	12,050	9,214
1868	18,125	8,065
1869	13,733	3,207
1870	17,428	4,665
1871	10,208	5,064
1872	31,215	6,564
1873	33,892	4,461
1874	9,508	1,726
1875	13,140	4,947

The countries to which we sent British-grown hops, in 1875, were as follows:

	Quantities.	Value.
	cwts.	£
To Belgium	1,200	7,437
„ United States	1,075	8,108
„ Bombay and Scinde	497	3,640
„ Bengal and Burmah	695	4,699
„ Australia	7,848	50,038
„ other countries	1,825	12,769
	13,140	86,691

The proportion of hops used in making beer varies; beers for keeping or storing will have 2 lbs. to 3 lbs. to 22 gallons to ensure their keeping. For ordinary beer 1¾ to 2 lbs. will be used. Small beer, or table beer, will contain only the washing from hops which have served to prepare strong beer.

In 1863, the amount charged for brewers' licences, in

the United Kingdom, was 934,829*l.*, and in 1871 it was 399,576*l.*

There are no returns of the quantity of hops used by the brewers of the United Kingdom, but if we estimate them to average 2 lbs. per barrel, it would have taken 547,296 cwt. for the beer brewed in 1873, for home consumption and export, nearly one-half of which would in all probability have been imported.

In 1871, when upwards of 15 per cent. less beer was produced, 201,398 cwt. of hops were imported, chiefly from Germany, the United States, Belgium, and Holland; the exports during the same year amounting to 15,300 cwt.

Exports of Beer and Ale from the United Kingdom.

In 1826 the shipments were 53,013 barrels; in 1828, 59,471; and in 1830, 74,902 barrels. Since 1840, the annual exports have been as follows:

	Barrels.		Barrels.
1840	174,618	1858	533,828
1841	148,099	1859	614,136
1842	141,313	1860	584,827
1843	146,339	1861	378,461
1844	169,830	1862	464,827
1845	156,743	1863	491,631
1846	133,383	1864	498,981
1847	134,005	1865	561,907
1848	136,724	1866	564,176
1849	135,692	1867	518,838
1850	182,480	1868	496,646
1851	190,077	1869	495,110
1852	244,115	1870	521,199
1853	416,422	1871	483,120
1854	308,941	1872	522,080
1855	384,414	1873	584,939
1856	410,392	1874	599,413
1857	435,334	1875	504,511

BEER STATISTICS AND MALT CONSUMPTION.

The following figures give the proportionate consumption of malt per head of the population in the United Kingdom, in bushels:

1840	1·59	1852	1·48	1864	1·75		
1841	1·34	1853	1·49	1865	1·74		
1842	1·32	1854	1·29	1866	1·82		
1843	1·30	1855	—	1867	1·67		
1844	1·34	1856	1·48	1868	1·73		
1845	1·30	1857	1·58	1869	1·71		
1846	1·49	1858	1·59	1870	1·84		
1847	1·25	1859	1·67	1871	1·72		
1848	1·34	1860	1·45	1872	1·93		
1849	1·40	1861	1·61	1873	1·98		
1850	1·47	1862	1·50	1874	1·94		
1851	1·46	1863	1·67	1875	—		

Consumption of Beer.—According to a statement published by M. Gustave Noback, during the Vienna Exhibition of 1873, the following is the proportional consumption of beer per head of the population in the leading countries. The first and second columns represent millions, as we have omitted the figures for hundreds. The litre, it may be stated, is equivalent to about 1¾ pint.

	Population.	Total Consumption.	Proportion per Head.
		litres.	litres.
Austria and Hungary	35,644	1,222,200	34·50
Prussia	24,693	927,190	39·60
Saxony	2,556	154,528	60·50
Other parts of Northern Germany	4,116	200,299	48·50
Bavaria	4,198	920,703	219·00
Wurtemberg	1,818	280,108	154·00
Baden	1,461	41,895	56·00
Alsace-Lorraine	1,638	83,631	51·00
Great Britain and Ireland	30,838	3,568,259	118·00
Belgium	4,829	700,000	145·00
France	36,103	700,000	19·00
Netherlands	3,652	135,572	37·00
Sweden	4,159	52,000	14·50
Norway	1,701	25,340	12·50
Russia	63,659	974,000	14·00
North America	38,650	998,200	26·00

BEER STATISTICS AND MALT CONSUMPTION. 133

According to this estimate, the Bavarians and Belgians are the greatest beer drinkers, and after them come the English. In France and some other countries of Europe a great deal of beer is surreptitiously brewed, so that the proportions are scarcely reliable.

Number of licences granted to brewers in the United Kingdom, duty charged, and barrels of beer brewed:

	No. of Licences.	Duty.	Barrels of Beer brewed.
		£	
1854	45,294	85,330	..
1855	43,176	80,247	..
1856	41,570	76,968	..
1857	41,326	78,474	17,984,773
1858	40,741	79,796	18,166,635
1859	40,519	78,794	19,152,564
1860	40,388	80,992	20,340,096
1861	39,680	81,231	19,534,460
1862	38,829	78,067	19,989,313
1863	38,376	302,668	20,081,408
1864	39,508	314,382	21,360,461
1865	38,261	332,851	22,546,889
1866	38,249	344,803	25,388,600
1867	38,125	378,691	25,206,665
1868	36,737	357,597	24,301,841
1869	35,664	355,672	24,542,664

1854 is for year ending the 5th January; the later years end 31st March.

It is curious to note the gradual decrease in the number of brewers, from 45,000 to about 30,000 at the present time, which indicates the centralization of the trade in the hands of large firms. The proportion of brewers in the different divisions of the kingdom in 1869 was as follows: England, 35,287; Scotland, 249; Ireland, 128.

In the year ending March 31, 1873, there were in the

United Kingdom the following number of brewers, maltsters, and dealers, as shown by the amount paid for licences:

	England.	Scotland.	Ireland.	United Kingdom.
Brewers	30,671	226	113	31,010
Maltsters	4,434	400	143	4,997
Malt roasters and dealers	24	2	8	34
Dealers and retailers in beer	123,801	1,875	18,749	144,425

The following table gives the number of brewers in the United Kingdom in the year ending September 30, 1873, from which it will be seen that the bulk of the beer is brewed by some sixty large firms:

Brewers Brewing over	Brewers Brewing under	No. of Brewers.
barrels.	barrels.	
	1,000	24,416
1,000	10,000	1,894
10,000	20,000	234
20,000	30,000	82
30,000	50,000	63
50,000	100,000	34
100,000	150,000	9
150,000	200,000	6
200,000	250,000	1
250,000	300,000	2
300,000	350,000	2
350,000	400,000	1
400,000	700,000	5
Beginners		3,179
		29,929

From the above statistics, we are able to form a tolerably correct estimate of the capital and number of hands employed in the malting and brewing trade of the kingdom. Presuming that one man is able to malt 30 bushels per day, there must be about 12,000 men engaged in the manufacture of malt. In the cultivation of the barley, taking one man to 35 acres, there are employed about 70,000 men. In the cultivation of hops, taking one man to 5 acres, there are employed more than 12,000 men. In brewing, assuming that one man is required for every 500 barrels brewed, there must be employed about 135,000 men. There are about 145,000 dealers and retailers of beer in the United Kingdom, and many of these employ several hands as tapsters, cellarmen, &c. Taking into consideration all the accessory trades in connection with breweries, including engineers, coopers, carters, &c., there cannot be far short of half a million hands employed in this important industry, and the capital invested must reach the almost fabulous sum of 200,000,000*l*. The brewing and malting trades yield to the State for duty, licences, &c., a revenue of almost 10,000,000*l*.*

* Mr. T. A. Pooley, in 'British Manufacturing Industries.'

1884.

BOOKS RELATING

TO

APPLIED SCIENCE

PUBLISHED BY

E. & F. N. SPON,

LONDON: 16, CHARING CROSS.

NEW YORK: 35, MURRAY STREET.

A Pocket-Book for Chemists, Chemical Manufacturers,
Metallurgists, Dyers, Distillers, Brewers, Sugar Refiners, Photographers,
Students, etc., etc. By THOMAS BAYLEY, Assoc. R.C. Sc. Ireland, Analytical and Consulting Chemist and Assayer. Third edition, with additions, 437 pp., royal 32mo, roan, gilt edges, 5s.

SYNOPSIS OF CONTENTS:

Atomic Weights and Factors—Useful Data—Chemical Calculations—Rules for Indirect Analysis—Weights and Measures—Thermometers and Barometers—Chemical Physics—Boiling Points, etc.—Solubility of Substances—Methods of Obtaining Specific Gravity—Conversion of Hydrometers—Strength of Solutions by Specific Gravity—Analysis—Gas Analysis—Water Analysis—Qualitative Analysis and Reactions—Volumetric Analysis—Manipulation—Mineralogy—Assaying—Alcohol—Beer—Sugar—Miscellaneous Technological matter relating to Potash, Soda, Sulphuric Acid, Chlorine, Tar Products, Petroleum, Milk, Tallow, Photography, Prices, Wages, Appendix, etc., etc.

The Mechanician: A Treatise on the Construction and Manipulation of Tools, for the use and instruction of Young Engineers and Scientific Amateurs, comprising the Arts of Blacksmithing and Forging; the Construction and Manufacture of Hand Tools, and the various Methods of Using and Grinding them; the Construction of Machine Tools, and how to work them; Machine Fitting and Erection; description of Hand and Machine Processes; Turning and Screw Cutting; principles of Constructing and details of Making and Erecting Steam Engines, and the various details of setting out work, etc., etc. By CAMERON KNIGHT, Engineer. *Containing* 1147 *illustrations,* and 397 pages of letter-press. Third edition, 4to, cloth, 18s.

On Designing Belt Gearing. By E. J. COWLING
WELCH, Mem. Inst. Mech. Engineers, Author of 'Designing Valve Gearing.' Fcap. 8vo, sewed, 6d.

A Handbook of Formulæ, Tables, and Memoranda, for Architectural Surveyors and others engaged in Building. By J. T. HURST, C.E. Thirteenth edition, royal 32mo, roan, 5s.

"It is no disparagement to the many excellent publications we refer to, to say that in our opinion this little pocket-book of Hurst's is the very best of them all, without any exception. It would be useless to attempt a recapitulation of the contents, for it appears to contain almost *everything* that anyone connected with building could require, and, best of all, made up in a compact form for carrying in the pocket, measuring only 5 in. by 3 in., and about ¼ in. thick, in a limp cover. We congratulate the author on the success of his laborious and practically compiled little book, which has received unqualified and deserved praise from every professional person to whom we have shown it."—*The Dublin Builder.*

The Cabinet Maker; being a Collection of the most approved designs in the Mediæval, Louis-Seize, and Old English styles, for the use of Cabinet Makers, Carvers, &c. By R. CHARLES. 96 *plates,* folio, half-bound, 10s. 6d.

Quantity Surveying. By J. LEANING. With 42 illustrations, crown 8vo, cloth, 9s.

CONTENTS :

A complete Explanation of the London Practice.	Schedule of Prices.
General Instructions.	Form of Schedule of Prices.
Order of Taking Off.	Analysis of Schedule of Prices.
Modes of Measurement of the various Trades.	Adjustment of Accounts.
Use and Waste.	Form of a Bill of Variations.
Ventilation and Warming.	Remarks on Specifications.
Credits, with various Examples of Treatment.	Prices and Valuation of Work, with Examples and Remarks upon each Trade.
Abbreviations.	The Law as it affects Quantity Surveyors, with Law Reports.
Squaring the Dimensions.	
Abstracting, with Examples in illustration of each Trade.	Taking Off after the Old Method.
Billing.	Northern Practice.
Examples of Preambles to each Trade.	The General Statement of the Methods recommended by the Manchester Society of Architects for taking Quantities.
Form for a Bill of Quantities.	
Do. Bill of Credits.	Examples of Collections.
Do. Bill for Alternative Estimate.	Examples of "Taking Off" in each Trade.
Restorations and Repairs, and Form of Bill.	Remarks on the Past and Present Methods of Estimating.
Variations before Acceptance of Tender.	
Errors in a Builder's Estimate.	

A Practical Treatise on Heat, as applied to the Useful Arts; for the Use of Engineers, Architects, &c. By THOMAS BOX. With 14 *plates.* Third edition, crown 8vo, cloth, 12s. 6d.

A Descriptive Treatise on Mathematical Drawing Instruments : their construction, uses, qualities, selection, preservation, and suggestions for improvements, with hints upon Drawing and Colouring. By W. F. STANLEY, M.R.I. Fifth edition, *with numerous illustrations,* crown 8vo, cloth, 5s.

*Spons' Architects' and Builders' Pocket-Book of Prices
and Memoranda.* Edited by W. YOUNG, Architect. Royal 32mo, roan, 4s. 6d.; or cloth, red edges, 3s. 6d. *Published annually.* Eleventh edition. Now ready.

Long-Span Railway Bridges, comprising Investigations of the Comparative Theoretical and Practical Advantages of the various adopted or proposed Type Systems of Construction, with numerous Formulæ and Tables giving the weight of Iron or Steel required in Bridges from 300 feet to the limiting Spans; to which are added similar Investigations and Tables relating to Short-span Railway Bridges. Second and revised edition. By B. BAKER, Assoc. Inst. C.E. *Plates,* crown 8vo, cloth, 5s.

Elementary Theory and Calculation of Iron Bridges and Roofs. By AUGUST RITTER, Ph.D., Professor at the Polytechnic School at Aix-la-Chapelle. Translated from the third German edition, by H. R. SANKEY, Capt. R.E. With 500 *illustrations,* 8vo, cloth, 15s.

The Builder's Clerk: a Guide to the Management of a Builder's Business. By THOMAS BALES. Fcap. 8vo, cloth, 1s. 6d.

The Elementary Principles of Carpentry. By THOMAS TREDGOLD. Revised from the original edition, and partly re-written, by JOHN THOMAS HURST. Contained in 517 pages of letterpress, and *illustrated with* 48 *plates and* 150 *wood engravings.* Third edition, crown 8vo, cloth, 18s.

Section I. On the Equality and Distribution of Forces — Section II. Resistance of Timber — Section III. Construction of Floors — Section IV. Construction of Roofs — Section V. Construction of Domes and Cupolas — Section VI. Construction of Partitions — Section VII. Scaffolds, Staging, and Gantries — Section VIII. Construction of Centres for Bridges — Section IX. Coffer-dams, Shoring, and Strutting — Section X. Wooden Bridges and Viaducts — Section XI. Joints, Straps, and other Fastenings — Section XII. Timber.

Our Factories, Workshops, and Warehouses: their Sanitary and Fire-Resisting Arrangements. By B. H. THWAITE, Assoc. Mem. Inst. C.E. *With* 183 *wood engravings,* crown 8vo, cloth, 9s.

Gold: Its Occurrence and Extraction, embracing the Geographical and Geological Distribution and the Mineralogical Characters of Gold-bearing rocks; the peculiar features and modes of working Shallow Placers, Rivers, and Deep Leads; Hydraulicing; the Reduction and Separation of Auriferous Quartz; the treatment of complex Auriferous ores containing other metals; a Bibliography of the subject and a Glossary of Technical and Foreign Terms. By ALFRED G. LOCK, F.R.G.S. *With numerous illustrations and maps,* 1250 pp., super-royal 8vo, cloth, 2l. 12s. 6d.

CATALOGUE OF SCIENTIFIC BOOKS

Progressive Lessons in Applied Science. By EDWARD
SANG, F.R.S.E. Crown 8vo, cloth, each Part, 3s.
Part 1. Geometry on Paper—Part 2. Solidity, Weight, and Pressure—Part 3. Trigonometry, Vision, and Surveying Instruments.

A Practical Treatise on Coal Mining. By GEORGE
G. ANDRÉ, F.G.S., Assoc. Inst. C.E., Member of the Society of Engineers.
With 82 *lithographic plates.* 2 vols., royal 4to, cloth, 3*l.* 12*s.*

Sugar Growing and Refining: a Comprehensive
Treatise on the Culture of Sugar-yielding Plants, and the Manufacture, Refining, and Analysis of Cane, Beet, Maple, Milk, Palm, Sorghum, and Starch Sugars, with copious statistics of their production and commerce, and a chapter on the distillation of Rum. By CHARLES G. WARNFORD LOCK, F.L.S., &c., and G. W. WIGNER and R. H. HARLAND, FF.C.S., FF.I.C. *With* 205 *illustrations,* 8vo, cloth, 30*s.*

Spons' Information for Colonial Engineers. Edited
by J. T. HURST. Demy 8vo, sewed.

No. 1, Ceylon. By ABRAHAM DEANE, C.E. 2*s.* 6*d.*

CONTENTS:
Introductory Remarks—Natural Productions—Architecture and Engineering—Topography, Trade, and Natural History—Principal Stations—Weights and Measures, etc., etc.

No. 2. Southern Africa, including the Cape Colony, Natal, and the Dutch Republics. By HENRY HALL, F.R.G.S., F.R.C.I. With Map. 3*s.* 6*d.*

CONTENTS:
General Description of South Africa—Physical Geography with reference to Engineering Operations—Notes on Labour and Material in Cape Colony—Geological Notes on Rock Formation in South Africa—Engineering Instruments for Use in South Africa—Principal Public Works in Cape Colony: Railways, Mountain Roads and Passes, Harbour Works, Bridges, Gas Works, Irrigation and Water Supply, Lighthouses, Drainage and Sanitary Engineering, Public Buildings, Mines—Table of Woods in South Africa—Animals used for Draught Purposes—Statistical Notes—Table of Distances—Rates of Carriage, etc.

No. 3. India. By F. C. DANVERS, Assoc. Inst. C.E. With Map. 4*s.* 6*d.*

CONTENTS:
Physical Geography of India—Building Materials—Roads—Railways—Bridges—Irrigation—River Works—Harbours—Lighthouse Buildings—Native Labour—The Principal Trees of India—Money—Weights and Measures—Glossary of Indian Terms, etc.

A Practical Treatise on Casting and Founding,
including descriptions of the modern machinery employed in the art. By N. E. SPRETSON, Engineer. Third edition, with 82 *plates* drawn to scale, 412 pp., demy 8vo, cloth, 18*s.*

Gas Works: their Arrangement, Construction, Plant,
and Machinery. By F. COLYER, M. Inst. C.E. With 31 *folding plates*,
8vo, cloth, 24*s*.

The Clerk of Works: a Vade-Mecum for all engaged
in the Superintendence of Building Operations. By G. G. HOSKINS,
F.R.I.B.A. Third edition, fcap. 8vo, cloth, 1*s*. 6*d*.

Tropical Agriculture; or, the Culture, Preparation,
Commerce, and Consumption of the Principal Products of the Vegetable
Kingdom, as furnishing Food, Clothing, Medicine, etc., and in their
relation to the Arts and Manufactures; forming a practical treatise and
Handbook of Reference for the Colonist, Manufacturer, Merchant, and
Consumer, on the Cultivation, Preparation for Shipment, and Commercial
Value, etc., of the various Substances obtained from Trees and Plants
entering into the Husbandry of Tropical and Sub-Tropical Regions. By
P. L. SIMMONDS. Second edition, revised and improved, 515 pages,
8vo, cloth, 1*l*. 1*s*.

American Foundry Practice: Treating of Loam,
Dry Sand, and Green Sand Moulding, and containing a Practical Treatise
upon the Management of Cupolas, and the Melting of Iron. By T. D.
WEST, Practical Iron Moulder and Foundry Foreman. Second edition,
with numerous illustrations, crown 8vo, cloth, 10*s*. 6*d*.

The Maintenance of Macadamised Roads. By T.
CODRINGTON, M.I.C.E, F.G.S., General Superintendent of County Roads
for South Wales. 8vo, cloth, 6*s*.

Hydraulic Steam and Hand Power Lifting and
Pressing Machinery. By FREDERICK COLYER, M. Inst. C.E., M. Inst. M.E.
With 73 *plates*, 8vo, cloth, 18*s*.

Pumps and Pumping Machinery. By F. COLYER,
M.I.C.E., M.I.M.E. With 23 *folding plates*, 8vo, cloth, 12*s*. 6*d*.

The Municipal and Sanitary Engineer's Handbook.
By H. PERCY BOULNOIS, Mem. Inst. C.E., Borough Engineer, Portsmouth. *With numerous illustrations*, demy 8vo, cloth, 12*s*. 6*d*.

CONTENTS.

The Appointment and Duties of the Town Surveyor—Traffic—Macadamised Roadways—Steam Rolling—Road Metal and Breaking—Pitched Pavements—Asphalte—Wood Pavements—Footpaths—Kerbs and Gutters—Street Naming and Numbering—Street Lighting—Sewerage—Ventilation of Sewers—Disposal of Sewage—House Drainage—Disinfection—Gas and Water Companies, &c., Breaking up Streets—Improvement of Private Streets—Borrowing Powers—Artizans' and Labourers' Dwellings—Public Conveniences—Scavenging, including Street Cleansing—Watering and the Removing of Snow—Planting Street Trees—Deposit of Plans—Dangerous Buildings—Hoardings—Obstructions—Improving Street Lines—Cellar Openings—Public Pleasure Grounds—Cemeteries—Mortuaries—Cattle and Ordinary Markets—Public Slaughter-houses, &c.—Giving numerous Forms of Notices, Specifications, and General Information upon these and other subjects of great importance to Municipal Engineers and others engaged in Sanitary Work.

6 CATALOGUE OF SCIENTIFIC BOOKS

Tables of the Principal Speeds occurring in Mechanical Engineering, expressed in metres in a second. By P. KEERAYEFF, Chief Mechanic of the Obouchoff Steel Works, St. Petersburg; translated by SERGIUS KERN, M.E. Fcap. 8vo, sewed, 6*d.*

Spons' Dictionary of Engineering, Civil, Mechanical, Military, and Naval; with technical terms in French, German, Italian, and Spanish, 3100 pp., and *nearly* 8000 *engravings,* in super-royal 8vo, in 8 divisions, 5*l.* 8*s.* Complete in 3 vols., cloth, 5*l.* 5*s.* Bound in a superior manner, half-morocco, top edge gilt, 3 vols., 6*l.* 12*s.*

See page 15.

A Treatise on the Origin, Progress, Prevention, and Cure of Dry Rot in Timber; with Remarks on the Means of Preserving Wood from Destruction by Sea-Worms, Beetles, Ants, etc. By THOMAS ALLEN BRITTON, late Surveyor to the Metropolitan Board of Works, etc., etc. *With* 10 *plates,* crown 8vo, cloth, 7*s.* 6*d.*

Metrical Tables. By G. L. MOLESWORTH, M.I.C.E. 32mo, cloth, 1*s.* 6*d.*

CONTENTS.

General—Linear Measures—Square Measures—Cubic Measures—Measures of Capacity—Weights—Combinations—Thermometers.

Elements of Construction for Electro-Magnets. By Count TH. DU MONCEL, Mem. de l'Institut de France. Translated from the French by C. J. WHARTON. Crown 8vo, cloth, 4*s.* 6*d.*

Electro-Telegraphy. By FREDERICK S. BEECHEY, Telegraph Engineer. A Book for Beginners. *Illustrated.* Fcap. 8vo, sewed, 6*d.*

Handrailing: by the Square Cut. By JOHN JONES, Staircase Builder. Fourth edition, *with seven plates,* 8vo, cloth, 3*s.* 6*d.*

Handrailing: by the Square Cut. By JOHN JONES, Staircase Builder. Part Second, *with eight plates,* 8vo, cloth, 3*s.* 6*d.*

Practical Electrical Units Popularly Explained, with *numerous illustrations* and Remarks. By JAMES SWINBURNE, late of J. W. Swan and Co., Paris, late of Brush-Swan Electric Light Company, U.S.A. 18mo, cloth, 1*s.* 6*d.*

Philipp Reis, Inventor of the Telephone: A Biographical Sketch. With Documentary Testimony, Translations of the Original Papers of the Inventor, &c. By SILVANUS P. THOMPSON, B.A., Dr. Sc., Professor of Experimental Physics in University College, Bristol. *With illustrations,* 8vo, cloth, 7*s.* 6*d.*

PUBLISHED BY E. & F. N. SPON. 7

*A Pocket-Book of Useful Formulæ and Memoranda
for Civil and Mechanical Engineers.* By GUILFORD L. MOLESWORTH, Mem. Inst. C.E., Consulting Engineer to the Government of India for State Railways. *With numerous illustrations*, 744 pp., Twenty-first edition, revised and enlarged, 32mo, roan, 6s.

SYNOPSIS OF CONTENTS:

Surveying, Levelling, etc.—Strength and Weight of Materials—Earthwork, Brickwork, Masonry, Arches, etc.—Struts, Columns, Beams, and Trusses—Flooring, Roofing, and Roof Trusses—Girders, Bridges, etc.—Railways and Roads—Hydraulic Formulæ—Canals, Sewers, Waterworks, Docks—Irrigation and Breakwaters—Gas, Ventilation, and Warming—Heat, Light, Colour, and Sound—Gravity: Centres, Forces, and Powers—Millwork, Teeth of Wheels, Shafting, etc.—Workshop Recipes—Sundry Machinery—Animal Power—Steam and the Steam Engine—Water-power, Water-wheels, Turbines, etc.—Wind and Windmills—Steam Navigation, Ship Building, Tonnage, etc.—Gunnery, Projectiles, etc.—Weights, Measures, and Money—Trigonometry, Conic Sections, and Curves—Telegraphy—Mensuration—Tables of Areas and Circumference, and Arcs of Circles—Logarithms, Square and Cube Roots, Powers—Reciprocals, etc.—Useful Numbers—Differential and Integral Calculus—Algebraic Signs—Telegraphic Construction and Formulæ.

Spons' Tables and Memoranda for Engineers; selected and arranged by J. T. HURST, C.E., Author of 'Architectural Surveyors' Handbook,' 'Hurst's Tredgold's Carpentry,' etc. Fifth edition, 64mo, roan, gilt edges, 1s.; or in cloth case, 1s. 6d.

This work is printed in a pearl type, and is so small, measuring only 2½ in. by 1¾ in. by ¼ in. thick, that it may be easily carried in the waistcoat pocket.

"It is certainly an extremely rare thing for a reviewer to be called upon to notice a volume measuring but 2½ in. by 1¾ in., yet these dimensions faithfully represent the size of the handy little book before us. The volume—which contains 118 printed pages, besides a few blank pages for memoranda—is, in fact, a true pocket-book, adapted for being carried in the waistcoat pocket, and containing a far greater amount and variety of information than most people would imagine could be compressed into so small a space. . . . . The little volume has been compiled with considerable care and judgment, and we can cordially recommend it to our readers as a useful little pocket companion."—*Engineering.*

Analysis, Technical Valuation, Purification and Use of Coal Gas. By the Rev. W. R. BOWDITCH, M.A. *With wood engravings,* 8vo, cloth, 12s. 6d.

A Practical Treatise on Natural and Artificial Concrete, its Varieties and Constructive Adaptations. By HENRY REID, Author of the 'Science and Art of the Manufacture of Portland Cement.' New Edition, *with 59 woodcuts and 5 plates,* 8vo, cloth, 15s.

Hydrodynamics: Treatise relative to the Testing of Water-Wheels and Machinery, with various other matters pertaining to Hydrodynamics. By JAMES EMERSON. *With numerous illustrations,* 360 pp. Third edition, crown 8vo, cloth, 4s. 6d.

Electricity as a Motive Power. By Count TH. DU MONCEL, Membre de l'Institut de France, and FRANK GERALDY, Ingénieur des Ponts et Chaussées. Translated and Edited, with Additions, by C. J. WHARTON, Assoc. Soc. Tel. Eng. and Elec. *With 113 engravings and diagrams,* crown 8vo, cloth, 7s. 6d.

The Gas Analyst's Manual. By F. W. HARTLEY,
Assoc. Inst. C.E., etc. With numerous illustrations. Crown 8vo,
cloth, 6s.

Gas Measurement and Gas Meter Testing. By
F. W. HARTLEY. Fourth edition, revised and extended. *Illustrated*,
crown 8vo, cloth, 4s.

The French-Polisher's Manual. By a French-
Polisher; containing Timber Staining, Washing, Matching, Improving,
Painting, Imitations, Directions for Staining, Sizing, Embodying,
Smoothing, Spirit Varnishing, French-Polishing, Directions for Re-
polishing. Third edition, royal 32mo, sewed, 6d.

Hops, their Cultivation, Commerce, and Uses in
various Countries. By P. L. SIMMONDS. Crown 8vo, cloth, 4s. 6d.

A Practical Treatise on the Manufacture and Distri-
bution *of Coal Gas.* By WILLIAM RICHARDS. Demy 4to, with *numerous*
wood engravings and 29 *plates*, cloth, 28s.

SYNOPSIS OF CONTENTS:

Introduction—History of Gas Lighting—Chemistry of Gas Manufacture, by Lewis
Thompson, Esq., M.R.C.S.—Coal, with Analyses, by J. Paterson, Lewis Thompson, and
G. R. Hislop, Esqrs.—Retorts, Iron and Clay—Retort Setting—Hydraulic Main—Con-
densers — Exhausters — Washers and Scrubbers — Purifiers — Purification — History of Gas
Holder — Tanks, Brick and Stone, Composite, Concrete, Cast-iron, Compound Annular
Wrought-iron — Specifications — Gas Holders — Station Meter — Governor — Distribution —
Mains—Gas Mathematics, or Formulæ for the Distribution of Gas, by Lewis Thompson, Esq.—
Services—Consumers' Meters—Regulators—Burners—Fittings—Photometer—Carburization
of Gas—Air Gas and Water Gas—Composition of Coal Gas, by Lewis Thompson, Esq.—
Analyses of Gas—Influence of Atmospheric Pressure and Temperature on Gas—Residual
Products—Appendix—Description of Retort Settings, Buildings, etc., etc.

Practical Geometry, Perspective, and Engineering
Drawing; a Course of Descriptive Geometry adapted to the Requirements of the Engineering Draughtsman, including the determination of
cast shadows and Isometric Projection, each chapter being followed by
numerous examples; to which are added rules for Shading Shade-lining,
etc., together with practical instructions as to the Lining, Colouring,
Printing, and general treatment of Engineering Drawings, with a chapter
on drawing Instruments By GEORGE S. CLARKE, Capt. R.E. Second
edition, *with* 21 *plates.* 2 vols., cloth, 10s. 6d.

The Elements of Graphic Statics. By Professor
KARL VON OTT, translated from the German by G. S. CLARKE, Capt.
R.E., Instructor in Mechanical Drawing, Royal Indian Engineering
College. *With* 93 *illustrations*, crown 8vo, cloth, 5s.

The Principles of Graphic Statics. By GEORGE
SYDENHAM CLARKE, Capt. Royal Engineers. *With* 112 *illustrations.*
4to, cloth, 12s. 6d.

The New Formula for Mean Velocity of Discharge
of Rivers and Canals. By W. R. KUTTER. Translated from articles in the 'Cultur-Ingenieur,' by LOWIS D'A. JACKSON, Assoc. Inst. C.E. 8vo, cloth, 12s. 6d.

Practical Hydraulics; a Series of Rules and Tables for the use of Engineers, etc., etc. By THOMAS BOX. Fifth edition, *numerous plates*, post 8vo, cloth, 5s.

A Practical Treatise on the Construction of Horizontal and Vertical Waterwheels, specially designed for the use of operative mechanics. By WILLIAM CULLEN, Millwright and Engineer., *With* 11 *plates*. Second edition, revised and enlarged, small 4to, cloth, 12s. 6d.

Aid Book to Engineering Enterprise Abroad. By EWING MATHESON, M. Inst. C.E. The book treats of Public Works and Engineering Enterprises in their inception and preliminary arrangement; of the different modes in which money is provided for their accomplishment; and of the economical and technical considerations by which success or failure is determined. The information necessary to the designs of Engineers is classified, as are also those particulars by which Contractors may estimate the cost of works, and Capitalists the probabilities of profit. *Illustrated*, 2 vols., 8vo, 12s. 6d. each.

The Essential Elements of Practical Mechanics; based on the Principle of Work, designed for Engineering Students. By OLIVER BYRNE, formerly Professor of Mathematics, College for Civil Engineers. Third edition, *with* 148 *wood engravings*, post 8vo, cloth, 7s. 6d.

CONTENTS:

Chap. 1. How Work is Measured by a Unit, both with and without reference to a Unit of Time—Chap. 2. The Work of Living Agents, the Influence of Friction, and introduces one of the most beautiful Laws of Motion—Chap. 3. The principles expounded in the first and second chapters are applied to the Motion of Bodies—Chap. 4. The Transmission of Work by simple Machines—Chap. 5. Useful Propositions and Rules.

The Practical Millwright and Engineer's Ready Reckoner; or Tables for finding the diameter and power of cog-wheels, diameter, weight, and power of shafts, diameter and strength of bolts, etc. By THOMAS DIXON. Fourth edition, 12mo, cloth, 3s.

Breweries and Maltings: their Arrangement, Construction, Machinery, and Plant. By G. SCAMELL, F.R.I.B.A. Second edition, revised, enlarged, and partly rewritten. By F. COLYER, M.I.C.E., M.I.M.E. *With* 20 *plates*, 8vo, cloth, 18s.

A Practical Treatise on the Manufacture of Starch, Glucose, Starch-Sugar, and Dextrine, based on the German of L. Von Wagner, Professor in the Royal Technical School, Buda Pesth, and other authorities. By JULIUS FRANKEL; edited by ROBERT HUTTER, proprietor of the Philadelphia Starch Works. *With* 58 *illustrations*, 344 pp., 8vo, cloth, 18s.

A Practical Treatise on Mill-gearing, Wheels, Shafts,
Riggers, etc.; for the use of Engineers. By THOMAS BOX. Third edition, *with* 11 *plates.* Crown 8vo, cloth, 7s. 6d.

Mining Machinery: a Descriptive Treatise on the Machinery, Tools, and other Appliances used in Mining. By G. G. ANDRÉ, F.G.S., Assoc. Inst. C.E., Mem. of the Society of Engineers. Royal 4to, uniform with the Author's Treatise on Coal Mining, containing 182 *plates,* accurately drawn to scale, with descriptive text, in 2 vols., cloth, 3*l.* 12*s.*

CONTENTS:

Machinery for Prospecting, Excavating, Hauling, and Hoisting—Ventilation—Pumping—Treatment of Mineral Products, including Gold and Silver, Copper, Tin, and Lead, Iron, Coal, Sulphur, China Clay, Brick Earth, etc.

Tables for Setting out Curves for Railways, Canals,
Roads, etc., varying from a radius of five chains to three miles. By A. KENNEDY and R. W. HACKWOOD. *Illustrated,* 32mo, cloth, 2s. 6d.

The Science and Art of the Manufacture of Portland
Cement, with observations on some of its constructive applications. With 66 *illustrations.* By HENRY REID, C.E., Author of 'A Practical Treatise on Concrete,' etc., etc. 8vo, cloth, 18s.

The Draughtsman's Handbook of Plan and Map
Drawing; including instructions for the preparation of Engineering, Architectural, and Mechanical Drawings. *With numerous illustrations in the text, and* 33 *plates* (15 *printed in colours*). By G. G. ANDRÉ, F.G.S., Assoc. Inst. C.E. 4to, cloth, 9s.

CONTENTS:

The Drawing Office and its Furnishings—Geometrical Problems—Lines, Dots, and their Combinations—Colours, Shading, Lettering, Bordering, and North Points—Scales—Plotting —Civil Engineers' and Surveyors' Plans—Map Drawing—Mechanical and Architectural Drawing—Copying and Reducing Trigonometrical Formulæ, etc., etc.

The Boiler-maker's and Iron Ship-builder's Companion,
comprising a series of original and carefully calculated tables, of the utmost utility to persons interested in the iron trades. By JAMES FODEN, author of 'Mechanical Tables,' etc. Second edition revised, *with illustrations,* crown 8vo, cloth, 5s.

Rock Blasting: a Practical Treatise on the means employed in Blasting Rocks for Industrial Purposes. By G. G. ANDRÉ, F.G.S., Assoc. Inst. C.E. *With* 56 *illustrations and* 12 *plates,* 8vo, cloth, 10s. 6d.

Surcharged and different Forms of Retaining Walls.
By J. S. TATE. *Illustrated,* 8vo, sewed, 2s.

*A Treatise on Ropemaking as practised in public and
private Rope-yards*, with a Description of the Manufacture, Rules, Tables of Weights, etc., adapted to the Trade, Shipping, Mining, Railways, Builders, etc. By R. CHAPMAN, formerly foreman to Messrs. Huddart and Co., Limehouse, and late Master Ropemaker to H.M. Dockyard, Deptford. Second edition, 12mo, cloth, 3s.

Laxton's Builders' and Contractors' Tables; for the use of Engineers, Architects, Surveyors, Builders, Land Agents, and others. Bricklayer, containing 22 tables, with nearly 30,000 calculations. 4to, cloth, 5s.

Laxton's Builders' and Contractors' Tables. Excavator, Earth, Land, Water, and Gas, containing 53 tables, with nearly 24,000 calculations. 4to, cloth, 5s.

Sanitary Engineering: a Guide to the Construction of Works of Sewerage and House Drainage, with Tables for facilitating the calculations of the Engineer. By BALDWIN LATHAM, C.E., M. Inst. C.E., F.G.S., F.M.S., Past-President of the Society of Engineers. Second edition, *with numerous plates and woodcuts*, 8vo, cloth, 1l. 10s.

Screw Cutting Tables for Engineers and Machinists, giving the values of the different trains of Wheels required to produce Screws of any pitch, calculated by Lord Lindsay, M.P., F.R.S., F.R.A.S., etc. Cloth, oblong, 2s.

Screw Cutting Tables, for the use of Mechanical Engineers, showing the proper arrangement of Wheels for cutting the Threads of Screws of any required pitch, with a Table for making the Universal Gas-pipe Threads and Taps. By W. A. MARTIN, Engineer. Second edition, oblong, cloth, 1s., or sewed, 6d.

A Treatise on a Practical Method of Designing Slide-Valve Gears by Simple Geometrical Construction, based upon the principles enunciated in Euclid's Elements, and comprising the various forms of Plain Slide-Valve and Expansion Gearing; together with Stephenson's, Gooch's, and Allan's Link-Motions, as applied either to reversing or to variable expansion combinations. By EDWARD J. COWLING WELCH, Memb. Inst. Mechanical Engineers. Crown 8vo, cloth, 6s.

Cleaning and Scouring: a Manual for Dyers, Laundresses, and for Domestic Use. By S. CHRISTOPHER. 18mo, sewed, 6d.

A Handbook of House Sanitation; for the use of all persons seeking a Healthy Home. A reprint of those portions of Mr. Bailey-Denton's Lectures on Sanitary Engineering, given before the School of Military Engineering, which related to the "Dwelling," enlarged and revised by his Son, E. F. BAILEY-DENTON, C.E., B.A. *With* 140 *illustrations*, 8vo, cloth, 8s. 6d.

A Glossary of Terms used in Coal Mining. By
WILLIAM STUKELEY GRESLEY, Assoc. Mem. Inst. C.E., F.G.S., Member
of the North of England Institute of Mining Engineers. *Illustrated with
numerous woodcuts and diagrams*, crown 8vo, cloth, 5s.

A Pocket-Book for Boiler Makers and Steam Users,
comprising a variety of useful information for Employer and Workman,
Government Inspectors, Board of Trade Surveyors, Engineers in charge
of Works and Slips, Foremen of Manufactories, and the general Steam-
using Public. By MAURICE JOHN SEXTON. Second edition, royal
32mo, roan, gilt edges, 5s.

The Strains upon Bridge Girders and Roof Trusses,
including the Warren, Lattice, Trellis, Bowstring, and other Forms of
Girders, the Curved Roof, and Simple and Compound Trusses. By
THOS. CARGILL, C.E.B.A.T., C.D., Assoc. Inst. C.E., Member of the
Society of Engineers. *With 64 illustrations, drawn and worked out to scale*,
8vo, cloth, 12s. 6d.

A Practical Treatise on the Steam Engine, containing Plans and Arrangements of Details for Fixed Steam Engines,
with Essays on the Principles involved in Design and Construction. By
ARTHUR RIGG, Engineer, Member of the Society of Engineers and of
the Royal Institution of Great Britain. Demy 4to, *copiously illustrated
with woodcuts and 96 plates*, in one Volume, half-bound morocco, 2l. 2s.;
or cheaper edition, cloth, 25s.

This work is not, in any sense, an elementary treatise, or history of the steam engine, but
is intended to describe examples of Fixed Steam Engines without entering into the wide
domain of locomotive or marine practice. To this end illustrations will be given of the most
recent arrangements of Horizontal, Vertical, Beam, Pumping, Winding, Portable, Semi-
portable, Corliss, Allen, Compound, and other similar Engines, by the most eminent Firms in
Great Britain and America. The laws relating to the action and precautions to be observed
in the construction of the various details, such as Cylinders, Pistons, Piston-rods, Connecting-
rods, Cross-heads, Motion-blocks, Eccentrics, Simple, Expansion, Balanced, and Equilibrium
Slide-valves, and Valve-gearing will be minutely dealt with. In this connection will be found
articles upon the Velocity of Reciprocating Parts and the Mode of Applying the Indicator,
Heat and Expansion of Steam Governors, and the like. It is the writer's desire to draw
illustrations from every possible source, and give only those rules that present practice deems
correct.

Barlow's Tables of Squares, Cubes, Square Roots,
Cube Roots, Reciprocals *of all Integer Numbers up to* 10,000. Post 8vo,
cloth, 6s.

Camus (M.) Treatise on the Teeth of Wheels, demon-
strating the best forms which can be given to them for the purposes of
Machinery, such as Mill-work and Clock-work, and the art of finding
their numbers. Translated from the French, with details of the present
practice of Millwrights, Engine Makers, and other Machinists, by
ISAAC HAWKINS. Third edition, *with 18 plates*, 8vo, cloth, 5s.

A Practical Treatise on the Science of Land and

Engineering Surveying, Levelling, Estimating Quantities, etc., with a general description of the several Instruments required for Surveying, Levelling, Plotting, etc. By H. S. MERRETT. Third edition, 41 *plates with illustrations and tables*, royal 8vo, cloth, 12s. 6d.

PRINCIPAL CONTENTS:

Part 1. Introduction and the Principles of Geometry. Part 2. Land Surveying: comprising General Observations—The Chain—Offsets Surveying by the Chain only—Surveying Hilly Ground—To Survey an Estate or Parish by the Chain only—Surveying with the Theodolite—Mining and Town Surveying—Railroad Surveying—Mapping—Division and Laying out of Land—Observations on Enclosures—Plane Trigonometry. Part 3. Levelling—Simple and Compound Levelling—The Level Book—Parliamentary Plan and Section—Levelling with a Theodolite—Gradients—Wooden Curves—To Lay out a Railway Curve—Setting out Widths. Part 4. Calculating Quantities generally for Estimates—Cuttings and Embankments—Tunnels—Brickwork—Ironwork—Timber Measuring. Part 5. Description and Use of Instruments in Surveying and Plotting—The Improved Dumpy Level—Troughton's Level—The Prismatic Compass—Proportional Compass—Box Sextant—Vernier—Pantagraph—Merrett's Improved Quadrant—Improved Computation Scale—The Diagonal Scale—Straight Edge and Sector. Part 6. Logarithms of Numbers—Logarithmic Sines and Co-Sines, Tangents and Co-Tangents—Natural Sines and Co-Sines—Tables for Earthwork, for Setting out Curves, and for various Calculations, etc., etc., etc.

Saws: the History, Development, Action, Classification, and Comparison of Saws of all kinds. By ROBERT GRIMSHAW. With 220 *illustrations*, 4to, cloth, 12s. 6d.

A Supplement to the above; containing additional

practical matter, more especially relating to the forms of Saw Teeth for special material and conditions, and to the behaviour of Saws under particular conditions. *With* 120 *illustrations*, cloth, 9s.

A Guide for the Electric Testing of Telegraph Cables.

By Capt. V. HOSKIŒR, Royal Danish Engineers. *With illustrations*, second edition, crown 8vo, cloth, 4s. 6d.

Laying and Repairing Electric Telegraph Cables. By

Capt. V. HOSKIŒR, Royal Danish Engineers. Crown 8vo, cloth, 3s. 6d.

A Pocket-Book of Practical Rules for the Proportions

of *Modern Engines and Boilers for Land and Marine purposes*. By N. P. BURGH. Seventh edition, royal 32mo, roan, 4s. 6d.

Table of Logarithms of the Natural Numbers, from

1 to 108,000. By CHARLES BABBAGE, Esq., M.A. Stereotyped edition, royal 8vo, cloth, 7s. 6d.

To ensure the correctness of these Tables of Logarithms, they were compared with Callett's, Vega's, Hutton's, Briggs', Gardiner's, and Taylor's Tables of Logarithms, and carefully read by nine different readers; and further, to remove any possibility of an error remaining, the stereotyped sheets were hung up in the Hall at Cambridge University, and a reward offered to anyone who could find an inaccuracy. So correct are these Tables, that since their first issue in 1827 no error has been discovered.

14 CATALOGUE OF SCIENTIFIC BOOKS

The Steam Engine considered as a Heat Engine: a Treatise on the Theory of the Steam Engine, illustrated by Diagrams, Tables, and Examples from Practice. By JAS. H. COTTERILL, M.A., F.R.S., Professor of Applied Mechanics in the Royal Naval College. 8vo, cloth, 12s. 6d.

The Practice of Hand Turning in Wood, Ivory, Shell, etc., with Instructions for Turning such Work in Metal as may be required in the Practice of Turning in Wood, Ivory, etc.; also an Appendix on Ornamental Turning. (A book for beginners.) By FRANCIS CAMPIN. Third edition, *with wood engravings,* crown 8vo, cloth, 6s.

CONTENTS:

On Lathes—Turning Tools—Turning Wood—Drilling—Screw Cutting—Miscellaneous Apparatus and Processes—Turning Particular Forms—Staining—Polishing—Spinning Metals —Materials—Ornamental Turning, etc.

Health and Comfort in House Building, or Ventilation with Warm Air by Self-Acting Suction Power, with Review of the mode of Calculating the Draught in Hot-Air Flues, and with some actual Experiments. By J. DRYSDALE, M.D., and J. W. HAYWARD, M.D. Second edition, with Supplement, *with plates,* demy 8vo, cloth, 7s. 6d.

Treatise on Watchwork, Past and Present. By the Rev. H. L. NELTHROPP, M.A., F.S.A. *With 32 illustrations,* crown 8vo, cloth, 6s. 6d.

CONTENTS:

Definitions of Words and Terms used in Watchwork—Tools—Time—Historical Summary—On Calculations of the Numbers for Wheels and Pinions; their Proportional Sizes, Trains, etc.—Of Dial Wheels, or Motion Work—Length of Time of Going without Winding up—The Verge—The Horizontal—The Duplex—The Lever—The Chronometer—Repeating Watches—Keyless Watches—The Pendulum, or Spiral Spring—Compensation—Jewelling of Pivot Holes—Clerkenwell—Fallacies of the Trade—Incapacity of Workmen—How to Choose and Use a Watch, etc.

Notes in Mechanical Engineering. Compiled principally for the use of the Students attending the Classes on this subject at the City of London College. By HENRY ADAMS, Mem. Inst. M.E., Mem. Inst. C.E., Mem. Soc. of Engineers. Crown 8vo, cloth, 2s. 6d.

Algebra Self-Taught. By W. P. HIGGS, M.A., D.Sc., LL.D., Assoc. Inst. C.E., Author of 'A Handbook of the Differential Calculus,' etc. Second edition, crown 8vo, cloth, 2s. 6d.

CONTENTS:

Symbols and the Signs of Operation—The Equation and the Unknown Quantity—Positive and Negative Quantities—Multiplication—Involution—Exponents—Negative Exponents—Roots, and the Use of Exponents as Logarithms—Logarithms—Tables of Logarithms and Proportionate Parts — Transformation of System of Logarithms — Common Uses of Common Logarithms—Compound Multiplication and the Binomial Theorem—Division, Fractions, and Ratio—Continued Proportion—The Series and the Summation of the Series—Limit of Series—Square and Cube Roots—Equations—List of Formulæ, etc.

RECENTLY PUBLISHED.

In super-royal 8vo, 1168 pp., *with* 2400 *illustrations*, in 3 Divisions, cloth, price 13s. 6d. each; or 1 vol., cloth, 2l.; or half-morocco, 2l. 8s.

A SUPPLEMENT
TO
SPONS' DICTIONARY OF ENGINEERING,
Civil, Mechanical, Military, and Naval.

EDITED BY ERNEST SPON, MEMB. SOC. ENGINEERS.

THE success which has attended the publication of 'SPONS' DICTIONARY OF ENGINEERING' has encouraged the Publishers to use every effort tending to keep the work up to the standard of existing professional knowledge. As the Book has now been some years before the public without addition or revision, there are many subjects of importance which, of necessity, are either not included in its pages, or have been treated somewhat less fully than their present importance demands. With the object, therefore, of remedying these omissions, this Supplement is now being issued. Each subject in it is treated in a thoroughly comprehensive way; but, of course, without repeating the information already included in the body of the work.

The new matter comprises articles upon

Abacus, Counters, Speed Indicators, and Slide Rule.
Agricultural Implements and Machinery.
Air Compressors.
Animal Charcoal Machinery.
Antimony.
Axles and Axle-boxes.
Barn Machinery.
Belts and Belting.
Blasting. Boilers.
Brakes.
Brick Machinery.
Bridges.
Cages for Mines.
Calculus, Differential and Integral.
Canals.
Carpentry.
Cast Iron.
Cement, Concrete, Limes, and Mortar.
Chimney Shafts.
Coal Cleansing and Washing.

Coal Mining.
Coal Cutting Machines.
Coke Ovens. Copper.
Docks. Drainage.
Dredging Machinery.
Dynamo - Electric and Magneto-Electric Machines.
Dynamometers.
Electrical Engineering, Telegraphy, Electric Lighting and its practical details, Telephones
Engines, Varieties of.
Explosives. Fans.
Founding, Moulding and the practical work of the Foundry.
Gas, Manufacture of.
Hammers, Steam and other Power.
Heat. Horse Power.
Hydraulics.
Hydro-geology.
Indicators. Iron.
Lifts, Hoists, and Elevators.

Lighthouses, Buoys, and Beacons.
Machine Tools.
Materials of Construction.
Meters.
Ores, Machinery and Processes employed to Dress.
Piers.
Pile Driving.
Pneumatic Transmission.
Pumps.
Pyrometers.
Road Locomotives
Rock Drills.
Rolling Stock.
Sanitary Engineering.
Shafting.
Steel.
Steam Navvy.
Stone Machinery.
Tramways.
Well Sinking.

NOW COMPLETE.

With nearly 1500 *illustrations*, in super-royal 8vo, in 5 Divisions, cloth. Divisions 1 to 4, 13s. 6d. each ; Division 5, 17s. 6d. ; or 2 vols., cloth, £3 10s.

SPONS' ENCYCLOPÆDIA
OF THE
INDUSTRIAL ARTS, MANUFACTURES, AND COMMERCIAL PRODUCTS.

EDITED BY C. G. WARNFORD LOCK, F.L.S.

Among the more important of the subjects treated of, are the following :—

Acids, 207 pp. 220 figs.
Alcohol, 23 pp. 16 figs.
Alcoholic Liquors, 13 pp.
Alkalies, 89 pp. 78 figs.
Alloys.   Alum.
Asphalt.   Assaying.
Beverages, 89 pp. 29 figs.
Blacks.
Bleaching Powder, 15 pp.
Bleaching, 51 pp. 48 figs.
Candles, 18 pp. 9 figs.
Carbon Bisulphide.
Celluloid, 9 pp.
Cements.   Clay.
Coal-tar Products, 44 pp. 14 figs.
Cocoa, 8 pp.
Coffee, 32 pp. 13 figs.
Cork, 8 pp. 17 figs.
Cotton Manufactures, 62 pp. 57 figs.
Drugs, 38 pp.
Dyeing and Calico Printing, 28 pp. 9 figs.
Dyestuffs, 16 pp.
Electro-Metallurgy, 13 pp.
Explosives, 22 pp. 33 figs.
Feathers.
Fibrous Substances, 92 pp. 79 figs.
Floor-cloth, 16 pp. 21 figs.
Food Preservation, 8 pp.
Fruit, 8 pp.

Fur, 5 pp.
Gas, Coal, 8 pp.
Gems.
Glass, 45 pp. 77 figs.
Graphite, 7 pp.
Hair, 7 pp.
Hair Manufactures.
Hats, 26 pp. 26 figs.
Honey.   Hops.
Horn.
Ice, 10 pp. 14 figs.
Indiarubber Manufactures, 23 pp. 17 figs.
Ink, 17 pp.
Ivory.
Jute Manufactures, 11 pp., 11 figs.
Knitted Fabrics — Hosiery, 15 pp. 13 figs.
Lace, 13 pp. 9 figs.
Leather, 28 pp. 31 figs.
Linen Manufactures, 16 pp. 6 figs.
Manures, 21 pp. 30 figs.
Matches, 17 pp. 38 figs.
Mordants, 13 pp.
Narcotics, 47 pp.
Nuts, 10 pp.
Oils and Fatty Substances, 125 pp.
Paint.
Paper, 26 pp. 23 figs.
Paraffin, 8 pp. 6 figs.
Pearl and Coral, 8 pp.
Perfumes, 10 pp.

Photography, 13 pp. 20 figs.
Pigments, 9 pp. 6 figs.
Pottery, 46 pp. 57 figs.
Printing and Engraving, 20 pp. 8 figs.
Rags.
Resinous and Gummy Substances, 75 pp. 16 figs.
Rope, 16 pp. 17 figs.
Salt, 31 pp. 23 figs.
Silk, 8 pp.
Silk Manufactures, 9 pp. 11 figs.
Skins, 5 pp.
Small Wares, 4 pp.
Soap and Glycerine, 39 pp. 45 figs.
Spices, 16 pp.
Sponge, 5 pp.
Starch, 9 pp. 10 figs.
Sugar, 155 pp. 134 figs.
Sulphur.
Tannin, 18 pp.
Tea, 12 pp.
Timber, 13 pp.
Varnish, 15 pp.
Vinegar, 5 pp.
Wax, 5 pp.
Wool, 2 pp.
Woollen Manufactures, 58 pp. 39 figs.

London: E. & F. N. SPON, 16, Charing Cross.
New York: 35, Murray Street.

www.ingramcontent.com/pod-product-compliance
Lightning Source LLC
Chambersburg PA
CBHW030309170426
43202CB00009B/928